The Water-Thrifty Garden

Also by Stan DeFreitas

A Southern Gardener's Notebook (coauthor)
A Complete Guide To Florida Gardening

The Water-Thrifty Garden

Stan DeFreitas

Taylor Publishing Company
Dallas, Texas

Copyright © 1993 by Stan DeFreitas
The term XERISCAPE is trademark of the National Xeriscape Council, Inc.

Published by Taylor Publishing Company
1550 West Mockingbird Lane
Dallas, Texas 75235

Designed by Hespenheide Design
Botanical illustrations by Lynda Chandler
Photographs by Ann Wallace (unless otherwise indicated)

Library of Congress Cataloging-in-Publication Data
DeFreitas, Stan.
  The water-thrifty garden / Stan DeFreitas.
    p. cm.
    Includes index.
  ISBN 0-87833-793-8
    1. Xeriscaping. 2. Drought-tolerant plants. I. Title.
  SB475.83.D4 1993
  635.9'5—dc20   92-3982
                                             CIP
Printed in the United States of America
10 9 8 7 6 5 4 3 2 1

Contents

Acknowledgments

Many thanks to the National Xeriscape Council, Inc. and especially to Raymond Uecker, Jr., Executive Director, and Stephen J. Trudnak, who answered many questions and reviewed materials. Jack Wick and the California Association of Nurserymen also provided invaluable help with the western information in the book. I would also like to thank LaRue Robinson and Opal Schallmo of the Pinellas County Extension Service, Joan Bradshaw, Dr. Craig Chandler, and Dr. Michael Uhart of the National Weather Service.

Thanks to Lynda Chandler, the illustrator, for her wonderful plant renderings. The photographers did a great job as well: thanks to Ann Wallace, William D. Adams, Cynthia Woodyard, Scott Ogden, James Donovan, Walter Kingsley Taylor, William H. Allen, Jr., and Jerry Pavia. Jim Feinson, Ken Bagley, Sylvie Vidrine, and Gardener's Supply Company graciously contributed the irrigation system plan. The regional water-thrifty landscape plans are by Ursula Schultz, landscape design consultant— thanks for the fine work.

And, most importantly, thanks to my wife, Peggi.

INTRODUCTION: CONSERVING WATER IN YOUR GARDEN

With drought conditions prevalent from Florida to California, water-thrifty gardening is an idea whose time has come. In fact, many areas of the country have made water rationing mandatory. From community to city, to state, and even as a nation, we are learning to be more conservative with our most

precious resource, water. You may think that conserving water means that your landscape must look like a desert, but this doesn't have to be the case. Through knowledge and planning, water conservation can become an opportunity to have a *better* garden and landscape plan—a garden of color and beauty.

The population of our country is increasing at an enormous rate, especially in the warmer southern and southwestern states such as California, Texas, and Florida. We are constantly being told about drought conditions in our local papers, on television, and on the radio.

In many areas 5 to 6 inches of rain for the year may be the norm. Even in areas that receive 50 inches a year, drought conditions can still prevail within a few weeks because of the type of soil present.

Data indicates that we are using more water now than ever before. Since 1939, the national average for water consumption per person has risen 700 percent. Sometimes we have the mistaken impression that we have an endless supply of water, especially those of us living within a hundred miles of the coastline. Water, water everywhere . . . ? Well, present desalinization (the removal of salt) of ocean water is not happening on

This California garden boasts a beautiful pastel profusion of water-thrifty plants: the blue-violet rosemary, the silver artemisia, many daisies, and the shrub blue hibiscus, Alyogne huegelii.

a large scale, although some areas, such as Key West, Florida, have been desalting the ocean water for drinking and plant growth.

Because rainfall is so unpredictable and may vary dramatically from one geographic area to another, the amount of rain that falls at one time may make it seem as though there is enough rain for our needs. In fact, there may be too much rain in one place at one time, but because most soils cannot store the water adequately for a long time, there will often be water shortages during the typical dry season. We simply must conserve water.

As population increases in this country so does the demand for fresh water. By the year 2000, many areas will increase their water use from 20 to 30 percent. In general, there are a number of ideas to help stretch water needs. As you read further, you will find ideas to help make your garden and lawn tougher and able to sustain drier conditions.

THE SEVEN XERISCAPE PRINCIPLES

Xeriscape gardening is really very simple—it only involves a little do-ahead thinking. Here are the principles put together by the National Xeriscape Council.

"1. **Planning and Design:** Developing a landscape plan is the first and most important step in a successful Xeriscape landscape. A properly planned Xeriscape landscape takes into account the regional and micro climatic conditions of the site, existing vegetation and topographical conditions, the intended use and desires of the property owner, and the zoning or grouping of plant materials by their water needs. A landscape plan also allows landscaping to be done in phases. Many individuals can develop their own plan, but for best results, consult a landscape professional.

2. **Soil Analysis:** Soils will vary from site to site and even within a given site. A soil analysis based on random sampling provides information that enables proper selection of plants and any soil amendments needed. When appropriate, soil amendments can enhance the health and growing capabilities of the landscape by improving water drainage, moisture penetration and a soil's water-holding capacity.

3. **Appropriate Plant Selection:** Plant selection should be based on the plants' adaptability to the landscape area, the effect desired and the ultimate size, color, and texture of the plants. Plants should be arranged to achieve the aesthetic effect desired and grouped in accordance with their respective water needs. Most plants have a place in Xeriscape landscape. Maximum water conservation can be achieved by selecting the plants that require a minimal amount of supplemental watering in a given area. Landscape professionals can be of assistance when selecting plant material.

4. **Practical Turf Areas:** The type and location of turf areas should be selected in the same manner as all other plantings. Turf shouldn't be treated as a fill-in material but rather as a major planned element of the Xeriscape landscape. Since many turf varieties require supplemental watering at frequencies different than the other types of landscape plants, turf should be placed so it can be irrigated separately. While turf areas provide many practical benefits in a landscape, how and where it is used can result in a significant reduction in water use.

5. **Efficient Irrigation:** Watering only when plants need water and watering deeply encourages deeper root growth resulting in a healthier and more drought-tolerant landscape. If a landscape requires regular watering and/or if

an irrigation system is desired, the system should be well planned and managed. Water can be conserved through the use of a properly designed irrigation system. Consult landscape and irrigation professionals when planning irrigation for a Xeriscape landscape.

6. **Use of Mulches:** Mulches applied and maintained at appropriate depths in planting will assist soils in retaining moisture, reduce weed growth, and prevent erosion. Mulch can also be used where conditions aren't adequate or conducive for growing quality turf or ground covers. Mulches are typically wood bark chips, wood grindings, pine straws, nut shells, small gravel or shredded landscape clippings.

7. **Appropriate Maintenance:** Proper landscape and irrigation maintenance will preserve and enhance a quality Xeriscape landscape. When the first six principles have been followed, maintenance of a Xeriscape landscape is healthier and uses a minimal amount of water; less fertilizer, pesticides and other chemicals are needed to maintain the plant material."

—*Courtesy National Xeriscape Council, Inc.*

Fortunately, new varieties of plants, trees, and turf are being developed along with older varieties with proven drought tolerance. Research is under way to determine what native plants tolerate drought conditions. There are also new polymers that can be incorporated into the soil that may cut down water use as much as 70 percent. The actions that we take today, in both water conservation and landscaping, will definitely make our world a better place in the future.

In this book you will discover those plants that are more water conserving—perhaps they were there all along. This includes both native plants and introduced plants that may lend both beauty and strength to the garden. *The Water-Thrifty Garden* is also designed to help you learn that there are other alternatives to the large lawn and water-hungry plants that many of us have used in our traditional landscapes. A water-sensitive garden goes beyond the simple addition of mulch and soaker hoses; here you'll find landscape ideas that can be used in a new home or an existing one. Trees and groundcovers that are alternatives to common choices can help with energy conservation.

Your garden site and site analysis are discussed for planning a more efficient landscape and garden. From a simple planting plan to detailed drawings describing the overall concept of your water-thrifty landscape design, this book should help you with planning and installation. With minimal effort in most cases, less than you might have used in previous landscapes, you will find that although more thought may be needed, less time and money will be spent in maintaining a drought-tolerant garden.

Water-efficient landscaping and Xeriscape concepts offer beautiful design, low maintenance, and environmentally suitable techniques for both the novice grower and the enthusiastic gardener.

DROUGHT-TOLERANT LANDSCAPING

No matter the name—water-thrifty gardening, drought-tolerant landscaping, or Xeriscape gardening—the key is proper planting of the right tree, shrub, groundcover, or lawn. The best means for conserving water is to design and modify the landscape in order to reduce water requirements.

"Xeriscape" gardening is a new concept in the landscaping industry for planting with water conservation in mind, and it has quickly taken hold. It is derived from the Greek word *xeros* meaning "dry." Xeriscape-type landscapes were introduced by the Denver, Colorado, Water Department in 1981, although it was inspired by the gardening traditions of Spain, North Africa, and the Mideast, and by the natural landscapes of the Southwest.

MISUNDERSTOOD XERISCAPE CONCEPTS

"ALL DROUGHTS ARE THE SAME THROUGHOUT THE COUNTRY."

Of course, this statement is incorrect. In some parts of California the rainfall may average six inches a year whereas Florida normally receives 50 inches a year, on average. Fifty inches sounds like a tremendous amount, but most of this rainfall comes within a short span of time during the hot summer months. With the sandy soils that dry out quickly, droughts can occur in a short period of time. Long-term droughts have occurred over a number of years in some areas of Texas and in the Midwest.

"ALL XERISCAPE DESIGNS LOOK ALIKE."

No. Think instead of a fingerprint: no two look exactly the same. Choosing the right plant for its location will be different throughout the country—your landscape design does not have to be a "desert" with only cacti and rocks. Most of us think that cacti are the only plants that require little water, but there are many other plants that might be the right one for a particular site. Actually, desert plants can rot during a summer rainy season if good drainage is not present. The problem is that there seems to be a relative handfull of plants that all landscapers lean towards using in each region of the country. Many of these plants are water-ravenous and make each landscape appear similar to any other. We now see that removing our native plants and replacing them with exotic plants—especially imports from countries whose climate is different from ours—is foolish. There should be a *balance:* natural, native flora, wildlife habitats, along with native trees and shrubs—as well as *adapted* plants.

"I Don't Have to Water Drought-Tolerant Plants."

All new plantings need water on a regular basis until they are well established. Many of us have the misconception that drought-tolerant plants can be placed into the ground and then forgotten. In most cases, if 50 to 75 percent of the irrigation used is reduced, we will be successful in lower water-use gardening.

"I'll Have to Get Rid of My Lawn."

Practical reduction in turf grass areas is one of the goals of Xeriscape landscapes, but do not totally eliminate your turf area. Picking the *correct* species of turf for the site can make the difference in watering levels. Bahia and Bermuda are good choices for non-irrigated areas; although they may brown considerably during a severe drought, these grasses will green back up after the first rains. New varieties of St. Augustine, such as FX 10, and Buffalograss also appear to be good choices in some parts of the South.

Research done in the western part of the United States indicates that 1000 square feet of turf can use a third more water than a 15 × 30-foot swimming pool with a 5-foot deck around it. The reason for this is the pool has a liner that will not allow water to continuously drain through the soil. In my own pond, I have found that water lilies and natural plantings of Louisiana iris not only add beauty but also help to reduce the evaporation of water.

"Rocks Are a Good Mulch."

Many people think that having a lot of rocks and mulch in the landscape is good Xeriscape design. Rocks are not normally the best selection for mulching material. They increase the heat around your home (part of the "microclimate"), which raises your electric bill, and, of course, rocks do not give any organic matter back into the soil, which makes them environmentally ineffective.

"I'll Have to Replace All My Plants With Native American Plants."

Having all native plants isn't always the best choice in a water-conserving plan for the landscape. Some native plants are from dry, sandy soils, while others have been taken from wetland soils. Obviously, these plants cannot be dramatically placed into a foreign soil or condition. In one California test garden 8 out of 9 of the best drought-tolerant plants were non-natives, but were from areas with climates similar to that of the California test garden.

These misconceptions are examples of why people often do not choose the water-thrifty design approach as an alternative to the traditional landscape. This book will help to shatter some of these myths and offer a pleasurable, efficient, water-conserving way to landscape and garden.

> You can save an estimated 30 to 50 percent of the water normally being used through proper plant selection, mulching, addition of organic matter, and soil amendments such as some of the polymers.

DESIGNING YOUR
WATER-THRIFTY GARDEN

The word "design" needn't make you panic—it simply implies taking a thoughtful look at and approach to your landscape. When you're trying to save water and resources, "design" means anything from replacing portions of your turf area with an equally attractive groundcover to adding all new plantings of drought-tolerant plants. What's important is to evaluate your needs and wishes in a garden against what nature has given you, in terms of rainfall, soil, sun/shade, etc. This chapter discusses the kinds of design/planning principles you'll need to work with to create a water-thrifty garden.

This is the time to decide what your ideal garden and landscape should evolve into. What function do you want the landscape to provide? Is it for a play area, or more for visual enjoyment? Think about the activities you and your family enjoy, such as vegetable gardening, playing lawn games, suntanning, or entertaining. Will you need a utility area for a potting shed, firewood, storing lawn equipment such as lawn mowers, edgers, etc., or for maintaining the family RV (recreational vehicle)? Make a checklist of such areas you may have to incorporate into the landscape plan.

Privacy is also a factor to consider. Decide how much privacy you will need. You might want both public and private areas, for example, an entertaining (public) or family picnic (private) area. In many parts of the country, we can extend our home to the outside. Many people spend a great deal of their time outdoors. Pool areas with decking can become outside living rooms.

Here is a soft look, with the silvery foliage complementing the predominantly purple theme. The plants include two santolinas, S. chamaecyparis *and* S. virens, *and* Salvia *'Alan Chickering.'*

Finally, consider "traffic" patterns to and from the home or to areas where equipment is stored. When developing a design, you'll want to make sure such traffic is unobstructed. Lawns are very important in activity areas because of their wear resistance, yet they are also one of the highest water-use areas in the landscape. While it may not be necessary to totally eliminate the lawn area, reducing its size will help water conservation. There are some areas in the Southwest, however, where *no* lawn at all makes sense. Groundcovers and mulch may be sufficient for surviving the intense heat and lack of natural rainfall. (See the chapter on plant selection.)

EVALUATING YOUR SITE

Before drawing a plan or making any decisions, take a closer look at the special features/problems of your yard or garden. One important first factor is

Cynthia Woodyard

This Portland garden offers a bright mix of native plants and herbs: lavenders, yucca (foreground), yellow coreopsis, potentilla, and brilliant red monarda.

locating telephone and utility lines to avoid any major problems. In most areas of the country, call the local telephone or power company and they will be glad to tell you where your lines are located. As more developed and convenient services become available, more lines will run underground. Don't risk running into these.

This is also the time to check your soil. Check the drainage: how well does water percolate through the existing soil? Determine the type of soil you have (sandy, loamy, or clay in base?) and its compactness (will it need aeration?). Check the pH of the soil during site analysis. The term pH describes the acidity or alkalinity of the soil. You may find that some kind of soil improvement is needed. "Improving Your Soil"

explains more about soils and how to improve them.

Look at your property at different times during the day to find the areas where shade or sun is most prevalent. Is there shade on the east, west, or south side of the home? Shade obviously will make a big difference in the kind of plant material you select. As for plant material, first decide if you want to plant more trees, and where. Given their potential impact in the landscape—and their expense—you can't leave this decision until the last minute. Evaluate the plants you already have. What plants in the existing landscape are attractive and growing well—with a minimum amount of water? What features in your landscape might work better? Are there those tell-tale areas where irrigation is not quite getting the job done?

THE WEATHER

Besides looking at your existing site and plants, you have existing weather patterns to work with. You don't have to become a meteorologist, but you should be ever mindful of your local climatic conditions. How much annual rainfall does your area normally receive? Also, the frost dates, the seasonal temperatures, the prevailing winds, and how much cloud or fog cover should all be examined. Your water-thrifty landscape will rely upon plants that live and endure in your local climate. Often plants that are native to your particular area or plants from parts of the world with a climate similar to yours will rank highly in your selection of plants for the landscape.

CREATING A DESIGN

First, determine what you want to keep in the existing landscape based on the evaluations you've made. And when deciding on your landscape design, you may want to make sure that the landscape will be in harmony with your neighborhood. Other areas which need harmony are between the house and garden, or other plantings.

PROPORTION

Consider the proportion of the landscape, which is the mix of both plant material and structural material. This begins with the home, when you determine its proportion to the landscape. When choosing shrubs and trees, think of their ultimate sizes and shapes. Although trees are sometimes young when first planted into the landscape, they will ultimately grow to their maximum size and height with a spreading ability. Does the plant flow or will it climb over the wall? How does its growth effect the overall view of the landscape? These factors must be remembered when proportioning the landscape.

BALANCE

Balance is also a part of landscaping and should be part of your design plan. This could be through the use of color or the use of plants in mass. You could go for a visual weight. Often people place the same type of plant on either side of the walkway for a formal effect, although many gardeners today have steered away from formal landscapes in favor of naturalistic designs. Some of the informal styles are more subdued when using balance. In other words, a large oak tree to the right of the landscape might balance with a group of wax myrtles or crape myrtles on the left. You can also balance a concentration of colorful flowers such as lantana, marigolds, or portulacas in a bed against a patio on the other side of the house. Many people use groundcovers for a visual balance. But one

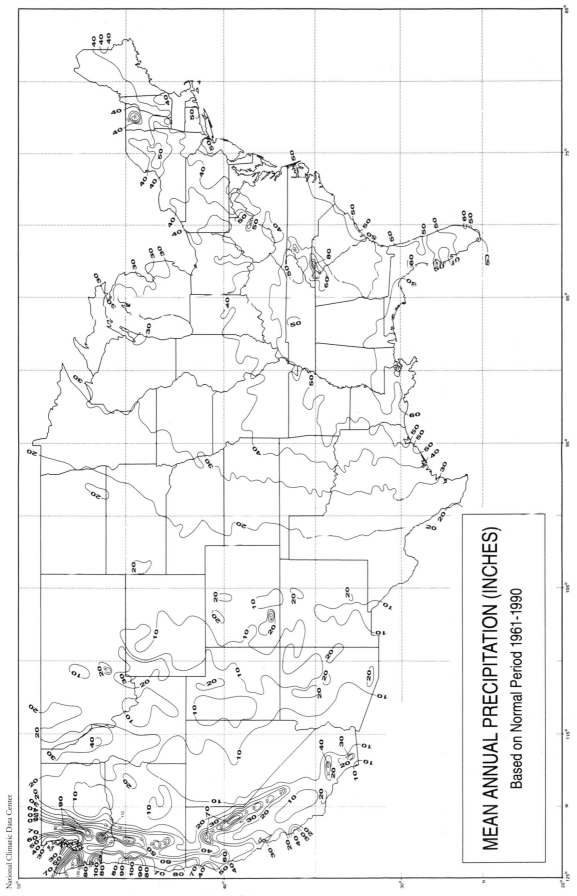

National Climatic Data Center

MEAN ANNUAL PRECIPITATION (INCHES)

Based on Normal Period 1961-1990

Annual precipitation (inches) in the United States.

pitfall when landscaping is to use the same landscape material over and over, or to make two symmetrical groupings. Remember, textures, shades, and shapes all have a way of making an important difference in the landscape.

UNITY

A landscape should be one unit rather than a number of areas coming together in a hodge-podge effect. You want to avoid the "Noah's Ark Effect," that is, two of everything: two roses, two hibiscus, two orange trees, two lemon trees, two palms . . . alas, too much! But you can use the same plant material in beds in repetition. Using groundcovers of the same type from one area of the landscape to another can bring unity, for example. Or use the same flowers, like strawflowers, geraniums, marigolds, or zinnias, to act as a unifying agent.

Often in the initial sketch of the landscape, the design can help bring unity into your landscape. Remember that you don't want the effect to look uncontrolled or like a jungle—unless you are going for that particular look. Also, remember that gardens change with the seasons. The magnolia tree is an attractive specimen with its beautiful large blossoms, but it is not so attractive when it is not in bloom and the leaves are coming down in the middle of your yard. Most flowering trees go through this. Maples and sweetgums are attractive trees when their foliage is changing colors. By the same token, they are not so attractive when it is time to rake all

of those leaves off of the deck or patio. Your swimming pool is a beautiful addition for the summer, but it is not quite as attractive in the middle of the winter season. Therefore, placement of trees, shrubs, and even pools should be thought of in terms of year-round landscaping. What you will change, what you will cover, and what you will rake all depends upon the overall unity or effect of the landscape.

Try not to have a Japanese rock garden with a French flower garden, along with a bed of bulbs from Holland. Any one of them can be effective, but remember that your yard is not an

HARDSCAPES

Many landscape architects use the concept of "hardscapes." This term refers to other alternatives rather than traditional landscape plants and materials. It does not mean that they do not use plant materials with water conservation in mind, but rather they incorporate the need for decking, gravel, stone, and wood into the landscape. Rather than a lawn, for example, a deck area can be used for playing and relaxing and bark or wood chips can be used to allow water-free movement—all somewhat less expensive than lawn maintenance. Many of these new materials can also keep the soil cool, which helps in the loss of evaporated water.

William D. Adams

Ornamental grasses offer good contrast to blooming ornamentals: here, purple fountain grass and black-eyed susans.

attraction where you have acres and acres of land to have different "themes." You can instead give different moods to different parts of the garden (if you have the space), linked by color scheme.

ZONES

Organizing the landscape into zones is not a new idea. It is a refreshingly sim- ple idea. Basically, when zoning the landscape you position plants together that use similar amounts of water. For example, problems can arise when impatiens and junipers (which use very little water) are planted in the same bed; both of these plants will find it difficult to survive, and one of these plants will eventually die. With zones, you make sure that every plant has the correct environment in its area. This environment includes water, soil, and sunlight. Junipers require less water, well-draining soil, and near full sun, while impatiens require a good deal of water, are tolerant of an improved soil, and need shade to partial sun depending upon the seasons. So, you would group these plants in areas with other plants of the same needs, say deeper rooted hollies with the junipers, or begonias or shallower rooted azaleas with the impatiens.

In planning a water-efficient landscape, be specific about the different existing zones. Break your landscape into zones, number them (1, 2, 3, 4, 5, etc.), and, after each zone, decide the water use in that particular area. This is a method used by many irrigation system designers. Your plan will break down into a high water-use zone (which is part of the landscape with plants needing the most water), including such plants as annual flowers, vegetable gardens, and turf areas. In your water-thrifty garden, keep this zone as small as possible to help reduce the extra water usage. In some parts of the country, especially in the west, people often speak of an oasis. Just as in desert conditions, the high water-use area (Zone 1) is normally very attractive, but for the most part, a small section of the landscape. This may be the part of the garden where wind and sun removes most of the moisture, an open area that perhaps is now your major turf area. Since this zone will probably have the attractive annuals, position it where you can enjoy it most—perhaps close to the house or a deck/patio area.

In moderate areas, or Zone 2, water is required, but not as much. The plants

The border of this Los Angeles garden designed by Chris Rosmini integrates Southwest native plants as well as plants from regions with a similar climate. In the front are silvery artemisias, white yarrows, yellow-blooming Santolina chamaecyparissus, *and the blue* Agapanthus *'Peter Pan.' The roses in the heart of the border are fed by drip irrigation, making more efficient the use of a typically water-thirsty plant.*

Cynthia Woodyard

here can take advantage of rains and possible runoff water from the house. This area is for plants not requiring constant watering, as opposed to those in the high-use zone. An occasional watering would probably be enough to get the plants in this area through a severe drought.

Zone 3, or the low-water-use area, is for plants that require the least amount of water or irrigation. Here, irrigation is only applied when first establishing the plantings. This could also be an area for native wildflowers, and native palms or trees. In other words, you want the plants here to get their water needs from the natural rainfall in your area—whether they be native plants or imported plants from regions which have climates similar to yours. Depending on the size of your garden, you can then continue with diminishing water-use zones, but three zones are really all you need to plan for.

THE OASIS AREA

A water-thrifty garden doesn't mean that you cannot use what are usually

This Florida oasis area features tropical plants such as bromeliads.

Ann Wallace

thought of as water-thirsty plants, such as azaleas, camellias, roses, or others. The trick is to place these plants in areas where the most effective watering can be used and where these plants will *naturally* receive more water (the Zone 1 mentioned before). These oasis areas will be watered more often than the rest of the landscape, but, since these plants are concentrated in the same area, you will not be wasting water. In a more traditional garden, you have to water the entire yard often just to satisfy the demands of the water-hungry plants that are scattered throughout the yard.

Planning is the key to having successful oasis areas in your garden. You might note that most plants will require fairly good irrigation to become established after transplanting. (This may not be true of some cacti or succulents, however.) Plants such as *Ligustrum, Viburnum, Pittosporum,* and crape myrtle all require good irrigation upon initial planting, but, once established, their water requirements are much less.

have a north and south orientation. Most landscape architects will mark "north" on the landscape plan in order to show the orientation of the homesite. If you're not sure, get out your trusty Scout compass and figure this out as it pertains to your property, especially if you are at the starting phase of landscaping and the lot is wooded.

Many plants grow best in a specific exposure. Remember, the position of the sun changes during the year. A spot that started out sunny during the winter season might be shady in the summer. Also, note how much sun a particular part of the yard receives and how this same spot varies during different parts of the day. If it's shady, what kind of shade? Is this dense shade or dappled? Will it affect the type of plants that you have selected to grow? Will the tree need to be trimmed to allow more sunlight into that particular area? Finally, what type of trees can be planted to alter the light level that is present now? All of these questions should be considered when planning the orientation and placing your plants into the landscape.

PLANT ORIENTATION— NORTH/SOUTH

It is important in landscape planning, as well as in the installation and growth of plants, to make sure to check the plants' orientation to the landscape. When making your plan, it is a good idea to

THE ACTUAL PLAN

Having a drawn-out plan not only makes the job less tedious, but actually more enjoyable. And you can avoid ex-

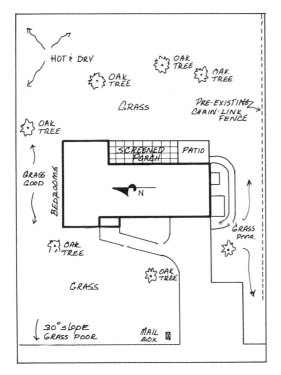

* NEED SHADE TOLERANT PLANTS UNDER OLD LIVE OAKS

The first step: what you have to work with.

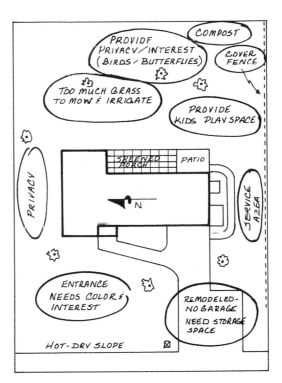

Then, defining your needs.

pensive mistakes down the road when you "see" them on paper.

On a large piece of graph paper draw your existing landscape. The original builder of your home will have a plot plan. From this, you can locate the property lines, the home's accesses (north, south, east, or west) and there may be other available information such as driveways, walkways, decks, or patios. On almost every landscape design, windows and entryways will be shown, along with the drainage patterns. To this plan, add the sunlight patterns, information about your soil's characteristics, and any other observations.

Place tracing paper over the graph paper once you have laid out the original design. Purchase a circle template and draw in trees and shrubs. Many people use a scale such as ¼ inch = 1 foot, 5 feet, 10 feet, or 20 feet, depending upon the size of the paper. Sketch several different designs, taking advantage of the drought-tolerant plants listed in the later chapters, allowing for creativity to flow. Experiment with some of the different Xeriscape ideas in this chapter.

You now have a blueprint for a great garden—your own!

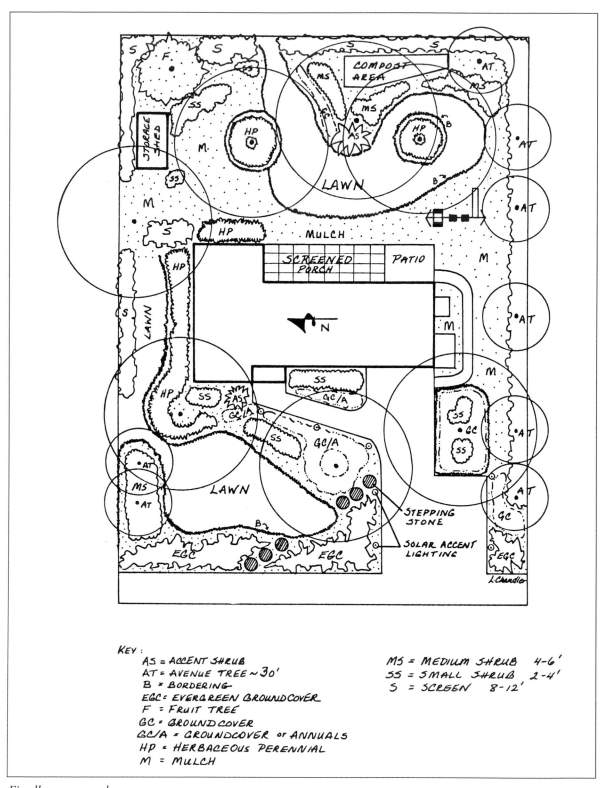

KEY :
   AS = ACCENT SHRUB
   AT = AVENUE TREE ~ 30'
   B = BORDERING
   EGC = EVERGREEN GROUNDCOVER
   F = FRUIT TREE
   GC = GROUNDCOVER
   GC/A = GROUNDCOVER or ANNUALS
   HP = HERBACEOUS PERENNIAL
   M = MULCH

MS = MEDIUM SHRUB   4-6'
SS = SMALL SHRUB   2-4'
S = SCREEN   8-12'

Finally, a master plan.

SAVING ENERGY—INCLUDING YOURS

Although most of this book is designed with water savings in mind, energy is among the resources that we must also try to save and manage wisely. Our need for energy continues to grow, yet it is not an unlimited commodity. In many areas, you can conserve energy simply by changing the climate around your home and surrounding property. We can save energy by managing outside water use in the garden and lawn, along with outdoor irrigation that can be reduced by Xeriscape landscape principles. Of course, reducing turf grass areas can be helpful. It has been estimated that our landfill sites are filled with about 30 to 50 percent of leaves, tree limbs and branches, or bark that could be used as compost, mulch, and soil builder. Recycling yard waste and water conservation go hand in hand in the wise use of energy, and it ultimately helps everyone.

Although you cannot change the climate in your particular area of the country, you can change the *microclimate*. This is a word used to define a smaller, more specific climatic area around houses that is influenced by more immediate elements. Changing the microclimate of the home and yard can result not only in a cooling of and increased comfort inside the home, but also—and more importantly—energy savings.

Energy conservation can be considered at the time the house is being built. But for many, the house has already been built, and you may want to "retro"-landscape the home (just a fancy way of saying that you will work within the existing landscape, maneuvering around plantings you wish to keep or can not move). Ideally, most houses would be more energy efficient if they were built with the long axis of the home running east to west, but this is not always geographically possible.

When landscaping try to choose trees that will help to improve the microclimate of your home. The shape, foliage, and size of the tree will be of particular interest in your consideration. Evergreen trees will hold their leaves year round. Deciduous trees can be planted closer to the house; the loss of their foliage in winter will allow sunlight through to heat the house. The south side of the house should get more direct sun during this period, which will allow for more heat during the winter months.

The density and shape of trees can also influence air movement. Trees may be tall and thin with branches growing close together, such as red cedar. If wind presents a problem, trees can be staggered in rows on the north side of the home to create a windbreak. Trees can be trimmed up to let the air flow around the base of the tree and first story of the home, but with the canopy left on the tree to help cool the roofs and walls of the home. Sometimes we forget that air circulation is important in obtaining the cooling effect we most desire for our home.

IMPROVING YOUR SOIL

We all know that soil is the structure for holding plants. It gives plants a medium to grow through. Soils vary considerably. Nursery plants are often started in soil-less mixtures, such as peat, perlite, vermiculite, and sand combinations. Research has also been done with plants that can grow in the air (called epiphytes) when given proper nutrients. These nutrients are sprayed, along with water, upon the leaves and roots. For most of us, soil has been definable in its use. Many soils will be composed of air, water, and both organic and inorganic particles. The organic material that was once living animal or plant tissue varies in amount. You can add more depending on your intent and need in the landscape.

If you dig down into your vegetable garden, you might find a cross section of different types of soil. The upper layer, or top soil, is normally darker in color and lighter in texture. This layer should also be easier to dig through than the lower layer, or subsoil. The top layer contains more organic matter (which is darker), giving it the ability to hold water and nutrients. In this upper layer you find higher amounts of plant hair roots, along with microorganisms that occur as well in the subsoil, even though many large trees and shrubs have dense, deep taproots. Earthworms—a healthy sign—can be found in many garden soils high in organic material. Plants send roots to the lower (sub)soil to bring up needed minerals and water.

SOIL TYPES

Soils also vary tremendously from one part of the country to the other. The particular type of top soil in your area may be light brown, brick red, or dark chocolate brown. The color helps indicate the kinds of minerals and clays the soil contains. The soil may be only an inch deep or a foot deep in some areas. Soils are normally classified according to the size of particles of which they are composed. The general types are sandy, clay, silty, or loamy.

In **sandy soils,** the particles are larger than in other soil types. The soil can be $\frac{1}{12}$ of an inch per particle size of the largest sand, to $\frac{1}{50}$ of an inch (medium sand), and $\frac{1}{250}$ of an inch in size (fine sand). Sand normally feels gritty to touch, and if you try to form a ball with sand, it normally falls apart upon release. For the landscape, use a course, builder-type sand for raised beds or making a potting soil mix. Sand mixed with clay makes an ideal soil.

With **clay soils,** the particles are minute. This soil consists of flattened particles that are tightly packed to allow little air or water movement. For this reason, clay soils are often called "heavy soils." When you try to form a ball with clay, it will normally maintain the shape. Clay feels slippery to the touch, does not crumble, and, because of its consistency, absorbs water very slowly, retaining the water and then releasing it.

Silt falls between clay and sand. Many gardeners describe their improved soil as a rich **loam.** Loam is a gardening term used to describe a soil that is a mix of sand, clay, and silt. Loam drains well but does not dry excessively. While water and nutrients can leach through it, loam normally holds them for longer periods of time, allowing the plant to use them as needed.

Soil Type	Depth reached by 1 inch of water
Sand	12 to 18 inches
Sandy Loam	8 to 15 inches
Loam	6 to 10 inches
Silt Loam	6 to 8 inches
Clay Loam	5 to 6 inches
Clay	3 to 6 inches

Soil Type	Water Infiltration Rate (inches per hour)
Sand	2.0
Sandy Loam	1.0
Loam	0.5
Silt Loam	0.4
Clay Loam	0.3
Clay	0.2

—*Texas Agricultural Extension Service*

THE IMPORTANT pH FACTOR

Determining the acidity or alkalinity of your soil is crucial to proper plant growth. The term "pH" indicates these characteristics, and is expressed in a scale from 0 to 14, with 7 being neutral. Any number below seven is acid, any number above seven is alkaline. Some peat soils have been tested with a pH factor of 4.0 to 4.2, which is very acidic, while very alkaline, shell-type, sandy soils have a pH factor of 8. It is wise to be concerned with the soil pH because this factor affects how different nutrients are used by the plant.

The pH factor of the soil can be tested at most County Extension Services or your local garden supply store. Every County Extension Service can provide instructions on how to send your sample to the appropriate testing site.

You can alter the pH factor of your soil from acid (sour) or alkaline (sweet). The best time to do this is when you are getting ready to relandscape or when just starting the new landscape. To counter an acidic soil, add lime. To counter an alkaline soil, add organic matter and use sulfur at 10 pounds per 1,000 square feet or soil acidifiers. And look for plants that thrive specifically in acidic or alkaline soils.

DRAINAGE

Water is the building block of life for plants, but "sitting" in water will kill most of them. Proper drainage should be a goal in your garden—to ensure that right balance of water retention.

You can correct a drainage problem as you put in a new garden design or redo the old one.

Most builders drain the water away from the home, but in many modern landscapes, designers drain the water into one part of the yard to help hold moisture there and to allow the water to percolate through existing soil. This is a better idea than running the water off into the street or sewer, since carried off with this runoff of water are traces of fertilizer or pesticides that can cause a problem for the environment. By forcing the water to accumulate on the property, surface runoff is minimized. And in a dry well area, water can collect and do a better job of keeping fertilizers and other materials in the soil where it is needed. If poorly drained areas are part of your landscape, you may need to slope or terrace the soil during the construction. In some cases, building a retaining wall will help to level off an area.

Clay soils, found in many areas around the country, can sometimes present a major problem, just as much as sandy soils do. Drainage is normally quite slow in deep clay soils. To help improve the water percolation and reduce runoff, mix extra amounts of organic matter into the soil. Raised beds are an option, especially for areas that have "hardpan." Hardpan is a tight, almost impervious layer of soil that causes water problems near the surface. Even if the top layer of soil allows the water to penetrate, hardpan is normally collected beneath and causes drainage problems. Of course, when a hardpan layer is fairly thin, you may be able to dig holes through it into the subsoil. These holes should be at least 12 inches in diameter. If the hardpan is too thick to dig through, then a raised bed garden is a good choice where an improved soil (peat, perlite, sand) or soil-less mixture can be added.

If the garden soil has been compacted due to construction or foot traffic, have the soil tilled down to a depth of 18 inches. This is especially helpful when different types of fill dirt are being brought to the site. Ideally, all fill should be at the same consistency. If the option exists, try not to buy different types of fill (sometimes called "top soil"). And any soil brought onto your property should be similar to the existing soils. If different types of soils are used, it will be more difficult for the soil to hold moisture. Also, labor and maintenance will be increased. If the soils are somewhat different, have the soils mixed by your nurseryman or landscape designer with a Rototiller.

ADDING ORGANIC MATTER

Just about every soil contains some organic matter in it, to one degree or another, organic matter being decomposed animal and plant tissue. Even the most sandy soils usually have a percent-

age of organic material. Of course, very few soils have perfect structure to begin with. In your garden or flower beds it is a good idea to improve the soil with extra organic matter. Organic matter is not applied just once and then forgotten about. Plants that are considered permanent landscape fixtures, such as trees, shrubs, and some woody perennials, will benefit from an organic mulch that can be placed around the root areas of these plants. As this mulch breaks down and decomposes, it will add more organic matter and nutrients, and give water-holding capacity to the soil.

There are a number of different sources of organic matter. Animal manures have been used for centuries and although hardly any of us live on a farm where this manure is readily available, animal manure, such as cow or chicken manure, can still be used to improve flower beds and most other landscape areas. The new processed chicken manure is most often used for lawn fertilization. Grass seems to grow at a very fast rate with this material.

Another source of organic matter is plant parts. In many landfills of the past, there could be 15% to 30%, perhaps up to 50%, of organic material. This includes leaves, stems, branches, and grass clippings, which will break down into a useful organic material for your garden. This material can also be used as a mulch, or you can allow the grass clippings from the mowers to fly. Along with grass clippings for mulch, you could use pine needles, tree leaves,

THE GARDEN COMPOST PILE

A compost pile merely mimics what Nature does itself, when decaying plant matter settles on the ground providing nutrients to new and established plants. You'll find that having your own compost heap benefits your garden and your pocketbook, as you improve soil with organic matter that you don't have to buy.

Locate your heap in a utility area of the garden that is also easily accessible—so you'll be more likely to keep attending to it. There are many pre-assembled bins and barrels available, or you can construct your own out of posts, slats, and wire, making a three-sided bin. The key is to provide air circulation to the heap, and gaps in the slats or using wire accomplishes this. Since you will be turning the materials in the heap, you'll also want to be able to do it conveniently.

There are many materials to go into your heap, the most common being those autumn leaves. Other garden waste works as well, but if there are large materials, be sure to shred them in some way, because the larger the matter, the longer it takes to break down. Kitchen wastes—tea bags, banana peels, vegetable scraps, rinds, eggshells, and much more—should also be a part of the mix. However, do not use animal parts, meat, pet manure, or grease. Layer the materials that you do use—leaves, soil, grass clippings, compost on hand, kitchen scraps, etc. There are "compost activators" available that will also get your heap going. Alfalfa meal is a good activator that is high in nitrogen. You should have enough piled up material so that the heap will generate heat. Water and turn the pile occasionally as well to hasten breakdown. Finished compost will be darker and a finer material than what you started with. Use your compost as potting soil or incorporate it into your garden soil.

chopped up branches, and shredded twigs. Many dedicated gardeners make compost piles using these materials. The by-products from this can be converted into a usable mulch or as a very good soil amendment.

Generosity is the key when adding organic matter. Mix all organic matter deeply and uniformly. Mix with a tilling device to bring aeration to the plants (aeration helps in overall growth).

Remember: an ideal soil will have 25% water and air, along with mineral and organic matter to make it desirable. Organic matter does have a disadvantage of being completely reduced by soil microorganisms and of course, rain, weather, and sunlight.

Add organic matter to vegetable gardens and annual beds at each planting time. Use 25 pounds of peat or organic material to 100 square feet. For permanent plantings, such as shrubs and trees, use 3 to 4 inches of an organic mulch over the top soil, which will help to conserve water and give the plants needed organic material when it breaks down. *Note:* Green or raw sawdust should be allowed to partially decompose before using. It might be necessary to add extra nitrogen to counter its loss, as the green sawdust starts to break down. When using a nitrogen source, one pound per 100 square feet is sufficient in countering these lost effects of sawdust.

There is a new material on the market, a potassium-based polymer. This can be applied to the soil before planting at one pound per 1000 square feet for new lawns and gardens. The polymer can be spread evenly with a seed spreader or by hand to allow a light blanket to cover the area. Cultivate this to a depth of 4 to 6 inches, placing the new sod or plants over this. Polymers have been used in existing lawns where watering was a problem and not only did they hold the water in the soil, but they had a life span of 5 to 7 years. This is a much better life span than other previously tested polymers. There are several brands of potassium-based polymers available; one I use is Hydrosol.

material to the garden. The addition of peat, grass clippings, leaves, coffee grounds, and banana peels (cut up in pieces) will benefit the growing process. Remember: All organic matter can be recycled. Also, the smaller the particle size, the quicker the breakdown will be into a more usable form. This is one reason why many people use shredders, lawn mowers, and even scissors to make leaves, clippings, and branches smaller.

HOW TO RETAIN WATER IN THE SOIL

Weeds are a major cause for water loss because they compete with your desired plants for water and nutrients. There are several weed mats that will help to hold water in the soil. Some products, like Weed Bloc®, are patented landscape fabrics that are waffled to allow air to flow through, yet conserve moisture and keep out weeds.

I can tell you from personal experience that weeding is one of my least favorite tasks in gardening. Any device that helps to save moisture and in the process keeps down weeds is a real bonus in my mind.

REPEATED APPLICATIONS

In growing fantastic flowers or in just having a good planting bed, repeat the application process of adding organic

MULCHES

Mulches are one of the best methods to help your soil hold water. Mulches are, quite simply, almost any substance that would cover over exposed garden soil or the area where you are putting in your landscape. There are, of course, many benefits to landscaping with mulches. These benefits include weed control, temperature control, and moisture conservation.

A good layer of mulch (3 to 4 inches thick) can help the soil surface retain moisture and not allow water to evaporate. This is very important during the long, dry summer when rainfall is rare. By using mulches, we make the most of the rainfall we get—and reduce the need for extra watering. Mulches hold water in an area where it might otherwise trickle down or run off to another area of the landscape.

A little known benefit of mulching is that it may help to keep the soil cooler in the summer and possibly a little warmer in the winter. The temperature of a mulched soil is more constant than that of an unmulched soil. This would allow the gardener to buffer temperature extremes. A mulch that keeps the soil cooler in the summer will prevent soil moisture from evaporating quickly. Earthworms seem to like soil that is not too hot or cold. Mulched areas of the garden seem to attract earthworms and other beneficial life in the soil.

There are many types of mulch. The most common are the shredded bark materials, such as cypress, redwood, pine bark, or other types of bark that are available in your area. You will want to shop around at your local nurseries and find out what materials are most recommended in your area. Many municipalities offer free recycled yard waste mulch to residents. Contact your local recycling department for more information.

Normally, a three-cubic-foot bag of material will cover about an 8-square-foot area about 2 to 3 inches deep. Of course, when using much of the organic type materials, such as wood and straw, you have to allow for the fact that the product will eventually break down. Some of the wood products will break down quicker than others. In some parts of California, redwood bark will be one of the longer lasting of the mulch material possibilities. By the same token, people who use sawdust or wood shavings find that these materials will break down quickly. Straw will also break down quickly. Other materials suitable for mulching are pine needles, which are often used in Florida, the mid-South, and some parts of California. They have a nice appearance and will normally last for years. Eventually, pine needles give a slightly acidic reaction to the soil, which is usually beneficial.

Another material that is often thought of in recycling is grass clippings. Many gardeners have the mistaken impression that grass clippings may cause odors and would not be a good mulch. My experience has been that grass clippings are an excellent mulch material and certainly a better alternative than using them to fill landfills. Tree leaves can also be used as a mulch. Oak, maple, and other leaves from deciduous trees are possibilities. Chop them up, moisten, and layer them around the plants.

Besides these true organic mulches, which are also returning nutrients to the soil as they break down, there are soil amendments that can also increase the plants' ability to thrive.

Inorganic materials can be used as mulches. There are many plastic "mulches." Weed-Bloc®, as mentioned previously, would be one of these. Polyethylene plastics, both clear and black, can be used. It may have a place in landscaping where water movement and air circulation is not needed, such as in rock gardens. Rocks are another mulch option, although one of the more porous materials such as bark would be a wiser choice. Many people still like the idea of using rocks. They are attractive as a permanent part of the landscape, and rocks do help to conserve moisture and can help keep weeds down. Different colored rocks and stones can actually complement the landscape. River rock and pea gravel can be used in certain situations and have a nice appearance. Inorganic mulches, however, generate heat, which is not usually a desired by-product!

FIGHTING EROSION

Erosion has become a major problem across the country due to natural and manmade causes. The loss of top soil has resulted in farmers losing farms, homesites being washed away, and, in general, a poorer quality of soil. We can prevent erosion by adding organic matter, by planting, and by covering the ground to hold the precious soil in place. The use of plants and trees can help to maintain the soil in the landscape and around the home.

A gardening concept often overlooked is cover crops. Up until now in this book, we have talked about planning for traditional garden plants, but sometimes we may wish to hold the soil in place before we get to our landscaping. Leaving soil exposed for long periods of time causes it to dry out and permits wind and rain to wash the soil away. If you do postpone your landscaping for any length of time, plant a cover crop—choosing a quick-growing plant that will cover and protect the area. Some gardeners have used cover crops for years, especially in vegetable gardening, and call them "green manures." These crops can be used in large garden areas. Many developers will use cover crops to help hold the soil before development. Some of the advantages to planting a cover crop are that the roots will grow into the soil to keep it loose and aerated, and, most importantly, to hold moisture in the soil. Many deep-rooted cover crops bring valuable minerals up to the top of the soil. This, of course, is especially important in vegetable gardening, but is also beneficial in the home or commercial landscape.

By holding the rainfall in check on your property, you will help to keep the soil from eroding. You will also keep perennial weeds from growing. Remember that in open, sun-drenched ground, weeds have a nasty habit of establishing themselves and taking over.

There are many plants that can be used in short-term cover crops. In landscape development, rye grass is often used as a cover. Winter rye or perennial rye, and, in some parts of the West and Midwest, alfalfa may be used. Annual rye is the better choice if you are going to put in a flower bed, as it will burn out as soon as the sun comes. Any cover crop should help to enrich the soil. Members of the pea family or legumes are the best. These plants help to enrich the soil through a process called nitrogen fixation. Little nodules that grow on the roots help to remove nitrogen from the air and make it available for other plants to use.

When you are ready to plant what you *really* want, simply till the cover crop with a Rototiller or add mulch or other organic material to be broken down into the soil.

PLANT SELECTION

Native Plants   Lawn Grasses   Vines and Groundcovers
The Water-Thirsty Plants

Plant selection—either for a new water-thrifty landscape or for an existing garden—probably seems intimidating. In this and the next few chapters, I offer a wide selection of drought-tolerant plants as well as new plant options to consider, such as using groundcovers in place of turf grasses. Increasingly, water-rationing and droughts

have created new demands for drought-tolerant plants and native plants. You'll find that your local nursery stocks such plants and is becoming knowledgeable about them. State agencies have the latest information on new, trustworthy plant varieties that can beat the heat and survive droughts. They are a valuable tool (see "Resources" for listings). Universities are usually the ones developing these new varieties, so you may find that your local university has information for the public. The variety of exciting and colorful water-thrifty plants is amazing, so have fun with a new plant.

USING NATIVE PLANTS

A native plant is an indigenous plant, a plant on the North American continent that has already adapted to its particular environment—the plains of the Midwest, the coastal South, the arid Southwest, etc.—and has survived without human care. Yaupon holly, flowering dogwood, annual and perennial sunflowers, black-eyed susan, live oak, and purple coneflower are only a few examples of the plants native to this continent.

In recent years, more people have considered using native plants in their

Cenizo (Texas Sage), an attractive native shrub.

gardens in order to get a natural, free-form look. In some areas, local and state governments are requiring that a certain percentage (perhaps 30% or 40%) of the landscape be done with plants native to that particular area. There are literally thousands of species of trees, shrubs, and flowering plants that are native to your area. Because the United States has an abundance of landscape material, these native plants should be a part of our residential, public, and commercial landscaping.

Native plants will adapt to local conditions much better than a plant brought in from other areas with different climates. Many of us assume that every native plant will do well in any situation. Unfortunately, this is not true. Now that more native plants are sold in local nurseries, your local nurseryman will be able to explain the requirements of the plant and what conditions will best suit it. The following chapters will also mention a plant's required conditions.

Today, builders with insight for the future will often leave native trees and shrubs in the landscape whenever possible. This is a far cry from past tradition, when builders simply bulldozed a building site completely and relandscaped with asphalt and new plant material. Native species will flourish, and sometimes introduced plants may not establish themselves and, often, die.

You might also save money by selecting native plants over the more expensive exotic species. Even though the costs may be similar, native plants, in general, will live longer, so choosing native plants would be more cost efficient in the long run.

Many of the native plants have adapted over the thousands of years to the particular soil conditions of an area, such as sandy soil, clay, and difficult conditions that would be fatal to other plants. This is not to say that there are not many new species that are really beautiful and adapted in any landscape. These non-natives include the bird-of-paradise and crape myrtle, both of which are wonderful flowering examples. Actually, some wildflowers you see are not necessarily native; rather, they are European or other introduced species that have "escaped" into the countryside, grow wild and thrive there. In other words, they have naturalized. Some bulb plants have done this. Sweet Autumn Clematic, the white-flowered vine, has naturalized in portions of the Southeast.

And don't think that all native plants are drab and ugly—they're not. Some may provide color in the fall and winter, when other perennials resemble brown sticks. There's one other benefit to using native plants: wildlife usually depends upon native plants. By working with native material we are improving the area for wildlife, as well as developing areas for man. So you might be delighted to find animal visitors in your garden such as hummingbirds or butterflies.

The following plant chapters indicate which are native plants and, in general, to what part of the United States they are native.

THE WORLDWIDE VIEW

Besides the increasing attention that native plants are getting, gardeners can also look to other parts of the globe for inspiration—regions that have a similar climate to their own.

Some of the European and Japanese plants that have been popular in the past come from regions that get more rainfall than, say, California, and so we find ourselves having to water them often. Now we are seeing interesting plants from Africa, Australia, the Mediterranean, and other areas that hold promise for the water-thrifty garden.

YOUR LAWN AREA

Almost all of us have to make a decision about how much lawn we really want or need. There are a lot of factors to consider when choosing a lawn—including who's going to mow it!

In selecting your lawn area, you may decide you can reduce certain areas. In some cities and counties, because of deed restrictions and homeowner associations, lawns may be a requirement. In other areas, you might be permitted to reduce the lawn area or to landscape and remove the lawn completely. Think about where to cut back on the lawn area to reduce mowing requirements and about replacing it with decks, vegetable gardens, or other flowers or shrubs.

No matter how big your lawn area winds up to be, there are new hardy turf varieties available to cut down on water use.

DROUGHT-TOLERANT AND HARDY TURF VARIETIES

There are a number of different turf varieties to choose from. Part of your decision should be based upon the area of the country you are in, the amount of foot traffic your lawn area will receive, and the amount of sun or shade the lawn area will receive. In the South, for example, warm-weather grasses are more successful, and are characterized by a coarser texture and larger blade. Some of these grasses go off color, or brown, in the winter season.

One of the most popular Southern grasses is **St. Augustine.** This is a "runner type" grass commonly found in Southern California, Texas, and the South. Basically, it is very thick-bladed and can be difficult to mow. With only medium drought tolerance, St. Augustine has many varieties, including a newer, more drought-tolerant strain, FX-10. Some of the more common varieties are Floratam, and Floratine (Bitter Blue). The greatest value of the St. Augustine groups, however, is that some will survive in shady areas, where other types of grasses may die.

Another popular grass is **Bermuda,** which is a warm-season grass. These are popular grasses for golf courses and areas where high maintenance is not a problem. They are fine-textured grasses which brown off in the winter and are not at all shade tolerant, but do thrive in open, sunny areas with proper care.

Another popular Southern grass is **Bahia.** This is a coarse-textured grass and will send up seed heads about every four days during the growing season. In hot, dry, sunny areas, such as Florida,

Bahia is a good choice. Two varieties are Argentine and Pensacola.

Zoysia is another grass said to be quite good. It has a very fine texture, similar to Bermuda, but it tends to have problems with nematodes. Nematodes are microscopic eel-like worms which thrive in the warmer climates and destroy grasses through the roots. This grass also has problems with browning early in winter and is slow to recover from cold damage.

Buffalograss (*Buchloe dactyloides)* is a native grass—native up through the Great Plains areas, from the Dakotas and Montana, down to Texas and Mexico—that is quickly gaining popularity for its looks, toughness, and droughttolerance. It is a soft-looking bluegreen grass, although some new varieties have the bright green color that many people desire in a lawn. Only needs infrequent mowing; left unmowed it reaches 5 inches. Requires full sun. It has not done well in Florida, but is a good choice for the Plains states, parts of the Southwest and South. 'Prairie' is a variety getting a lot of attention for its drought-tolerance and has been tested on golf courses.

Most of these warm-season grasses can be purchased as sod. The St. Augustine varieties are also available in plugs.

The "cool season" lawn grasses will stay green in winter and are subject to stress in very hot weather. They can brown and die in drier weather. These are fine-textured grasses and should be mowed on the high side. These grasses start well from seed or sod. Grasses such as **Kentucky Bluegrass,** a European grass, are popular in northern areas of the country. In the seed mixture, Kentucky Bluegrass may make up as much as 50% of a cool season grass mix and may be a permanent grass in the North and a temporary winter cover in the South.

There is also Marion, an old standard. Grass mixtures may include these as well as Fescues. Fescues are better in the Midwest.

Winter Rye Grass is popular in northern areas. It is also popular in the South as an over-seeded grass. That is, the rye grass is seeded into the regular lawn for the winter. As the primary grass browns for the winter months, the rye will sprout and offer a nice green lawn for the cooler months. The rye grass will die out as the weather warms and the primary grass will again green up. This usually occurs about May of each year.

GROUNDCOVERS

Groundcovers are very important to the Xeriscape-type garden or water-thrifty landscape, offering an alternative to large turf areas. This is a large category of plants, and includes those plants which, by the nature of their growing habits, will cover the ground quickly and thoroughly. Often they are vines, herbaceous perennials, or even shrubs. Traditional lawns and annuals can be called groundcovers.

The whole idea of using groundcovers is to "cover over" ground areas which might otherwise be used in a non-productive manner. Certainly plant material is preferred to concrete or asphalt. Not that these "paved" areas don't have their place, and, in the broad sense, can be called groundcovers as well. However, I prefer a green, growing groundcover, myself!

Junipers make effective groundcovers.

Many plants will spread as ground-covers. These include ivy, creeping fig, and many of the daisy plants. Plants like cotoneaster can be used. The most common groundcovers are grasslike plants. These would be evergreen and perennial. Groundcovers can be quite varied.

Probably the most important factor in selection for your area is design. In California, you might use *Pachysandra* (Japanese Spurge), because it looks good throughout the year. In other parts of the country, like the Northeast, English ivy or liriope might be found. Many groundcovers can flower, such as lily-of-the-valley (northern U.S. or Midwest) or *Aglaonema* (the tropical areas). In parts of California, *Dichondra,* which is a broad-leafed plant, is treated as a groundcover/lawn grass. In still other parts of the country, plants such as forsythia (or Dwarf Forsythia) and prostrate pyracantha are popular as groundcovers. Also popular is wild ginger.

Groundcovers allow the gardener to "unite" one area of the landscape to another. For unity and variety, ground-covers make excellent "fillers." You can create unique effects by planting groundcovers: with berries (holly), flowers (daisies), and evergreen (dwarf juniper). Consider groundcovers for the texture, color, or the overall "feel" of the plant.

Groundcovers will allow you to make your focal point even stronger. It may be that you are encircling your large oak tree with a bed of dwarf azaleas, or per-haps a circle of groundcover around your favorite maple tree. Often seen are beds of ajuga used as an interesting groundcover. One has to admire the way gardeners use lilyturf in different patterns and shapes along with mulched areas, thereby "pulling" different species together in one unified landscape.

Certain groundcovers can be used for special occasions. Often groundcovers are used where other plants are difficult, if not impossible, to grow. One of these would be shady areas. With more and more of us planting trees for environmental improvement, we create shady areas where shrubs don't grow and lawn grasses get weak and spindly. There are many groundcovers that grow well in these shady areas. Some of these include creeping fig, aluminum plant, cast iron plant, pachysandra, ginger, and many more. Of course, you may find it necessary to get the pruning saw out to trim off the lower branches of the trees to allow just a bit more light through to the groundcovers below.

Liriope muscari.

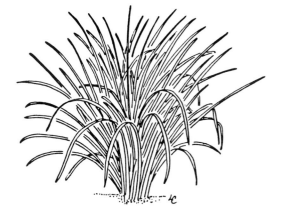

Often there will be difficult areas in the landscape where, for whatever reason, lawn grasses are not appropriate. In areas where the sun is quite bright, as in the Southwest, West, or Texas, you will want to use some sun-tolerant groundcovers. There are a number of varieties which work well. For full sun, periwinkles, dianthus (annual), ornamental grasses, or creeping Mediterranean herbs such as prostrate rosemary or native oreganos are good ones to start with.

There may be moist areas, where the soil is so damp that many plants just won't tolerate it well. Recommended are natural violets, mints (although they can be aggressive), and native ferns for these areas. Also try forget-me-nots or bunchberries.

In dry sites, where irrigation is difficult, some groundcovers such as thyme, pyracantha, or lavender will do very well. St. John's wort, shore juniper, or a dwarf holly would also do better in dry sites.

Groundcovers have often been used to cover over banks along creeks or brooks. If you have a very steep bank, and this is often the case with natural or manmade ponds, lawn grasses do not do well. Even if you could get lawn grasses to grow in these areas, mowing would be difficult. For banks, I have used dwarf juniper, creeping fig, ice plants, and even wild roses.

Some people like to use bulbs as groundcovers. You may think of this as a plant from Holland, such as the tulip, but there are many other bulbous plants which do well. Amaryllis makes a good groundcover in the warmer areas. Hyacinths do well in the cooler areas. Grape hyacinths often naturalize, giving their cheery deep purple color all across a meadow. Caladiums spread well and make an excellent groundcover. The caladium's beautiful multicolored foliage is attractive when mixed with blooming plants.

When using groundcovers, establish them in prepared soil, at a depth of about six inches. Bulbing plants especially prefer the addition of organic matter to the planting soil. Often, using several inches of mulch material seems to be beneficial as well.

In planting groundcovers, people often make the mistake of planting them too close together. Some of this depends upon how impatient you are for that desired effect. But, if you have large areas, you may wish to plant further apart; about one to three feet is ideal. It is rare to plant any closer than two feet (and many bulb plants will naturalize). Plant with some distance between the plants to allow them more room to spread. Using a weed-block material that allows water through, without allowing weeds to sprout, will be very beneficial (unless your groundcover spreads through underground means). For added protection, it is a good idea to mulch over the weed-block.

Groundcovers, by their very nature, propagate well. Most propagate with runners. This means they will slowly spread across an area. You may find that it is easy to take cuttings and peg the end into the ground to assist in rooting and spreading.

If you are planting on a bank or terrace, you may wish to erect burms of soil that will help to retain the moisture. While you are waiting for your plants or groundcovers to fill in, I recommend that you remove weeds by hand, or with an approved herbicide, such as Round-Up®. *If you do use a herbicide, you must read and follow the label directions carefully.* I have used groundcovers in many landscapes and find them to be a fine addition to water conservation or water-thrifty gardens.

Confederate Jasmine.

VINES

You can use vines in the landscape in much the same way you use groundcovers, and take advantage of the vertical interest they can give your garden. Vines are a versatile tool in the landscape and help to fill the air with beauty, color, and fragrance. Also, gardeners can turn an ugly chainlink fence or mail post into a thing of beauty just by the addition of a clinging flowering vine. Often vines can disguise an ugly view or utility building that you wish to hide. Porch columns are other areas where vines add a sky of color. While vines seem to have the problem of wandering throughout the garden (and Japanese honeysuckle comes to mind), this can also be an asset if managed properly. If you know the habits of the vine—in your garden—you can keep it under control and "train" it in the proper direction. When gardeners do have problems with vines, it is because they selected the wrong vines for the wrong location. Make sure the vine you select will survive your winter season and is suited for the amount of sunlight that is available. Many vines can be ornamental and functional, and are almost maintenance free.

Vines can be divided into two groups—do they climb or not? Vines with a climbing habit tend to grow vertically. They may choose to climb a tree or a trellis for support. Most vining plants have tendrils, small threadlike appendages that wrap around anything in their path. Tendrils are technically leaf stems. Grape vines are a good example of vines with tendrils. When a vine touches an object, such as a trellis or fence, it will start to move and climb around it. In some cases, gardeners will use wire mesh support, or, if it is handy, lattice will work as a satisfactory support. Nurseries stock lattice of different sizes and shapes so that vining plants will have a surface to climb on. I've even seen vining plants climb on chicken wire or construction wire, in fact grown as immediate topiaries in a landscape.

With some vines, you will find that they will not only hook onto the object, but actually start to adhere to it with an aerial root. This rootlet starts to burrow into the tiniest crack or crevice on which it is growing. This can be a problem if the surface is stucco or the wood side of your home. Heavy mantles of vines on your home trap moisture, a problem then for wood. If you do put a vine on your building, make certain that the building can support a vining plant without injury to the building or to the plant.

We may think of New England when we hear the term "ivy-covered halls," but English ivy and many other vines are happy in almost all parts of the country. Virginia creeper is considered a weed in some parts of the country, but it also makes a nice, naturalistic vining cover. The various clematis species have a wide distribution, contributing stun-

ning colors in almost every shade. There are so many vines, and I've listed the best drought-tolerant ones in the perennial chapter.

THE WATER-THIRSTY PLANTS

Why mention these? Well, they do have a place in the water-thrifty garden. After all, we all have soft spots for that special plant, be it roses, hydrangeas, azaleas, etc. The key again is planning. The more demanding plants belong in your oasis area, the area you've designated as having high water use. In fact, such special plants can have more of an impact in a tighter area. These are the plants that will benefit from a drip irrigation system (low volume) that provides controlled and specific watering. (See "Choosing a Water System.") Roses are probably the universal favorite—the rose is our national flower, after all— and I've given special instructions and varieties in the shrub chapter.

ꜟ꜠ ꜟ꜠ ꜟ꜠

You might find new, drought-resistant favorites, however, in the following chapters of specific plant listings. The appendix includes a cross-reference to the landscape plants listed, organized by regions of the country as well as by landscape use.

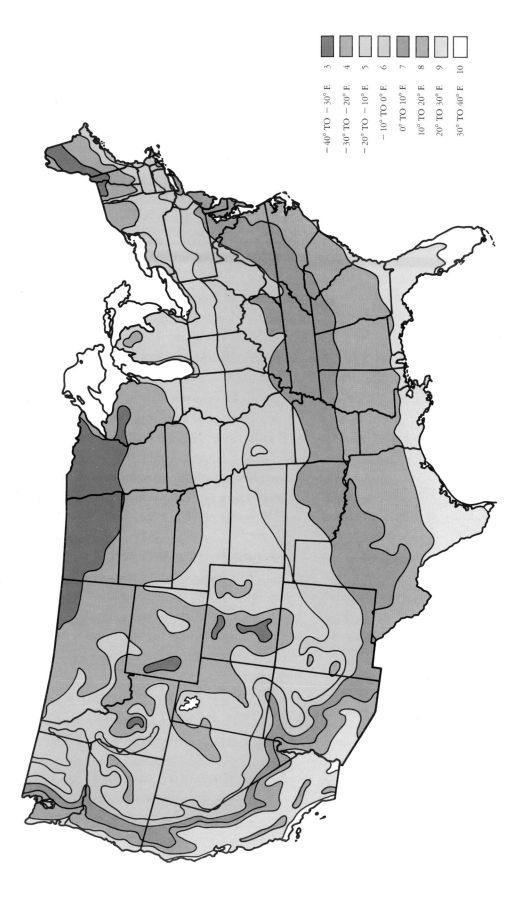

APPROXIMATE RANGE OF AVERAGE ANNUAL MINIMUM TEMPERATURES

−40° TO −30° F.	3
−30° TO −20° F.	4
−20° TO −10° F.	5
−10° TO 0° F.	6
0° TO 10° F.	7
10° TO 20° F.	8
20° TO 30° F.	9
30° TO 40° F.	10

Hardiness Zones of the United States.

DROUGHT-TOLERANT TREES

Choosing the correct tree is of paramount importance; trees are the backbone of your landscape. Selecting the wrong tree can also be a very costly mistake. Trees usually cost more than other landscape plants and have the most permanent effect on a garden's design. And because trees are slow growing, you may not recognize a poor choice for several years. When choosing a tree, you must consider its potential height, width, cold hardiness, and overall strength (to withstand wind storms, hurricanes, and lightning). You must also decide whether an evergreen, a deciduous, or a flowering tree is best for your landscape. To make your planning easier, we have compiled a list of the best drought-tolerant trees that will thrive in your garden—trees that will ultimately increase your property value and enhance the beauty of your landscape.

Acacia spp.

Some of the acacias are considered deciduous trees, but most are evergreen. The majority are kept as trees but a few varieties are shrubs. Many of these trees are native to the southwestern United States and other hot areas around the world. The leaves are finely cut on many species, yet some varieties have rough, course, flat leaves. The flowers are small, yellow to cream in color (some with bright yellow balls), and very showy. Many are fragrant. Acacias need good drainage. This plant shows signs of chlorosis when grown in a high range pH soil.

➤ *A. Baileyana,* 20 to 30 feet. This is a fast-growing evergreen from Australia with fragrant yellow flowers from winter through early spring.

William D. Adams

The gorgeous fall color of a native stand of Bigtooth Maple in the Texas Hill Country, the "Lost Maples," shows why this tree has become a popular landscape addition.

The dense, gray-blue foliage is finely divided. This particular variety can be seen growing mostly in California, and along the northwestern coast of the United States. Zone 8.

➢ *A. constricta,* Mescot Acacia, 18 to 20 feet. This shrub to small tree has feathery looking foliage. It requires little water. Native to Texas and Southwest. Zone 6.

THE NEW TREE IN THE LANDSCAPE AND TREE CARE

Heavy equipment is often used in building new landscapes, and soil compaction commonly occurs where such equipment is driven. As a result, one of the most important elements in an initial planting plan is soil compaction prevention. I recommend applying 6 inches of temporary mulch over the areas that heavy equipment will be driven on. Heavy boards or steel plates can be laid over the mulch for added protection. Most landscape designers designate off-limits areas with tree rings or wooden stakes (with yellow ribbon), to remind the equipment operators to keep clear.

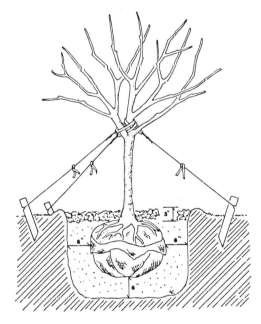

If possible, make sure that workers do not park their trucks and cars underneath your trees. This will also compact the soil and often the trees will decline in health, possibly dying after a few years. Because most of us pay a little extra for trees on the lot, it is important to save them, not only for economic reasons, but also to preserve the trees' ability to produce oxygen and shade for the landscape and home.

Establishing a new tree in the landscape. Note the three inches of mulch.

It is also important that you do not change the grade of the soil underneath the tree's canopy (the overhang of the branches). Many people pay extra for wooded lots only to alter the grade 6 inches or so, which effectively suffocates the tree's roots and eventually causes its death.

Look for tiny pin holes in the bark or sawdust on the trees. This indicates borers are present. When detected at an early stage, a certified pest control company should be called to treat the problem with the appropriate borer spray for trees. Trees in large groups usually have a greater chance for survival than do single specimen trees that have been injured. It is often wise to save the young, healthy trees in the landscape. If a tree has heart rot, or is heavily infested with borers or other diseases, the affected area should be removed. As a general rule, if over 10 percent of the tree turns brown, you could lose the tree. To increase your chances of maintaining a healthy tree, try to plant the longest-living trees, such as live oaks.

➤ *A. farnesiana,* Sweet Acacia, up to 20 feet. This deciduous tree has thorns with feathery, finely cut foliage. It has extremely fragrant, bright yellow flowers that bloom throughout the year. Native to Southwest and California. Zone 9.

➤ *A. longifolia.* This quick-growing, spreading shrub or small tree can reach heights of 20 feet. It too has yellow flowers and is normally used as a screening tree. Requires full sun. Has narrow foliage that is yellow-green in color. Zone 9.

➤ *A. minuta, A. smallii.* This tree resembles and is sometimes sold as the *farnesiana.* It can be seen growing mostly in the western part of the United States, California, Arizona, and Texas. Zone 8.

➤ *A. redolens,* 2 to 15 feet. This shrub to small tree makes an excellent spreading ground cover for very dry areas. (There is also a prostrate form available through Monrovia Nursery.) It requires full sun in order to produce its small, round puff of yellow flowers in the spring. It has sometimes been sold as *A. ongerup.* Zone 9.

➤ *A. saligna.* This fast-growing, evergreen tree has a weeping habit. It flowers with bright yellow clusters and requires full sun. Zone 9.

➤ *A. subporosa* 'Emerald Green,' up to 30 feet. This evergreen shrub to small tree has weeping branches with bright green foliage. It requires full sun for its round, yellow flowers. Zone 9.

Acer spp.
Maple

Most are deciduous trees that are drought-tolerant once they have been established.

➤ *A. Ginnala,* Amur maple. This is a small tree that can get to a height of 20 feet. With red, winged seeds. Very hardy. Native to the Rocky Mountain area. Zone 3.

➤ *A. glabrum,* Rocky Mountain maple. This is often a multi-trunked tree. Used more often in the Rocky Mountain area. Native to western Plains. Zone 5.

➤ *A. grandidentatum,* Bigtooth Maple, 30 to 40 feet. Native to Rocky Mountains and Southwest. Outstanding red and orange fall foliage. Zone 3.

➤ *A. palmatum,* Japanese maple, up to 20 feet. This small deciduous tree has a graceful habit of growth with great fall color. Grows well in partial shade. Zone 5.

➤ *A. rubrum,* 50 to 75 feet. This tree does well in boggy type soil, but can adapt to land areas if watered well to establish. An oasis area of the landscape would be best suited for this tree. Native to the East, but found all over the United States; cold-hardy up to Canada. Zone 4 or 5.

Aesculus californica
California Buckeye
25 feet
A large shrub to multi-trunked tree with a spreading habit of growth. The leaflets are 4 to 6 inches to 6 to 7 inches in length. The flowers are white to cream colored and candlelike. It requires full sun. The bright, shiny nuts that follow are inedible. This plant may drop its foliage in the summer if it is in a prolonged drought. Native to California. Zone 6.

Agonis flexuosa
Peppermint Tree
25 feet
This evergreen tree has a weeping habit. Small white flowers burst out in abundance. This tree becomes drought tolerant once it's established and likes full sun.

Albizia julibrissin
Mimosa, Silk Tree
30 feet
The mimosa is known for its powderpuff clusters of pink flowers in the spring. It has a moderately short trunk and a gently spreading canopy of soft, almost fernlike leaves. An excellent street or specimen tree. Once established, the mimosa grows well with only moderate waterings. Often escaped in Southeast. Zone 8.

Albizia Lebbeck
Woman's-Tongue Tree
50 feet
A large tree that can spread as wide as it is tall. It has pale green leaves with powderpufflike flowers in the spring that are pale yellow-green and 3 inches across. Woman's-Tongue grows in almost any soil and has good drought resistance. Zone 9.

Alnus rhombifolia
White Alder
50 to 90 feet
This deciduous tree can spread up to 40 feet. It requires full sun and takes both heat and drought well. Native to California and the Northwest. Zone 4.

Araucaria heterophylla
Norfolk Island Pine
This evergreen conifer has perfectly spaced tiers of horizontal branches. It is slow growing with fair drought tolerance once established. This tree requires full sun to partial shade. Zone 9 or 10.

Arborvitae spp., *Thuja* spp.
Up to 40 feet
This large, evergreen shrub or tree is columnar to globular in shape. Its foliage is dense, yellow to dark green in color

depending upon the variety. The tips of the foliage can turn a purple color in the fall. There are many varieties to choose from. It requires full sun for best growth. Water well when first establishing, then the plant becomes more drought tolerant. Zone 4 or 5.

Arbutus Unedo
Strawberry Tree
10 to 35 feet
This slow-growing, evergreen shrub or small tree has bark that is reddish brown and leaves that are dark green in color. It has small, white, urn-shaped flowers in the fall-winter season. Fruit from the past season is turning from yellow to orange-red in color that resembles the strawberry. The *Arbutus Unedo* is tolerant of many soils that drain well. It can take the desert heat in partial shade, to near full sun. Zone 6.

Bauhinia spp.
Orchid Tree
10 to 30 feet
A deciduous tree with blooms of white, purple, rose, or yellow, depending upon the species. The tree name comes from its orchid-shaped flowers. The orchid tree has fair drought tolerance once established. Zone 9–10.

Brachychiton populneus
Bottle Tree
This evergreen tree has a spreading growth habit of 30 to 60 feet. The trunk grows broad with age. This tree makes a good wind break or a screening plant. It can be adapted to desert conditions. The 3-inch leaves are egg-shaped and it has small, attractive cream colored flowers. This tree can develop root rot in wet soils of Texas and Florida. Zone 8.

Broussonetia papyrifera
Paper Mulberry
Up to 50 feet
This tree's spread can match its height. It has smooth gray bark on the trunk and the 5- to 8-inch leaves are heart-shaped. The paper mulberry can take the wind. It grows in many different soil types and suckers very well. Zone 6.

Bucida buceras
Black Olive
40 to 60 feet
A round, broad-headed tree with an upright trunk and drooping branches. It has leathery leaves, 2 to 4 inches long, and whorls on the tips of the branches. This graceful tree makes an excellent avenue or specimen tree in protected areas. Native to Florida and Mexico. Zone 10.

Bursera simaruba
Gumbo-Limbo Tree
60 feet
A large tree that can attain a width of about 40 feet. It has a stout trunk and deciduous leaves. Because of its size, it is most often used as a background or avenue planting. The gumbo-limbo has excellent salt tolerance as well as good drought tolerance, but it must be

planted where it will not freeze. Native to South Florida. Zone 10.

Caesalpinia spp.
(Poinciana)
10 to 30 feet

These evergreen or deciduous large shrubs or trees are fast growers. They are very drought tolerant after being established. The leaves are finely cut and feathery with flowers that are in clusters and have long, colorful stamens. One of these trees can take the desert heat of Arizona and the Southwest, as well as the heat of the South and Florida. It grows wild throughout these areas.

➢ *C. gilliesii,* Bird-of-Paradise, 10 feet. This fast grower has an upright, angular growth habit. The yellow flowers are 4 inches long with long, red stamens. It requires full sun to partial shade. Zone 8.

➢ *C. mexicana,* Mexican Bird-of-Paradise, 8 to 12 feet. This evergreen has yellow-green flowers throughout most of the year, excluding December, January, and February. Zone 9.

➢ *C. pulcherrima,* Dwarf Poincianna, 10 to 15 feet. Also known as the Barbados Pride, this deciduous shrub stays evergreen where the temperatures stay above freezing. It requires full sun to partial shade. The dwarf poincianna has attractive, reddish orange flowers that have long, red stamens. Even when

frozen, this plant comes back from the ground. Zone 9.

Callistemon spp.

➢ *C. citrinus,* Lemon Bottlebrush, 10 to 25 feet. This evergreen, small tree can be kept pruned to shrub form. It has narrow 2- to 4-inch leaves that are dense with bright red to crimson bottlebrush-shaped flowers in the spring. The woody seed capsules come later. The lemon bottlebrush grows well in many different types of soil and has good drought tolerance when established. It prefers full sun for best growth. Zone 9.

➢ *C. rigidus,* Stiff Bottlebrush, 5 to 20 feet. This evergreen tree has leaves from 2 to 5 inches long with red spikes of bottlebrushes. It can be used as a specimen plant. Place in full sun. Zone 9.

➢ *C. viminalis,* Weeping Bottlebrush, up to 20 feet. This evergreen shrub to small tree is willowy with bright red flowers. Water until established.

Caragana spp.
Pea Shrub
3 to 20 feet

These deciduous, small trees or shrubs have small leaflets and yellow, sweetpea-like flowers. The Siberian plant is tough and can withstand many conditions—deserts to mountains. Zone 3.

Cassia artemisioides
Feathery Cassia
4 to 6 feet
This large shrub to small tree has an open habit with needlelike, gray foliage and fragrant, yellow flowers. It prefers full sun. Zone 8.

Casuarina spp.
Australian Pine
Up to 60 feet
This leafless, evergreen tree has horsetaillike branches that are dark green in color with small brown cones. Sometimes used as a clipped hedge where it does not freeze. The Australian pine can be seen growing as a roadside hedge or windbreak seaside planting with some species. It requires full sun and takes the dry, summer conditions and desert areas. In some areas of Florida this pine is considered a weed tree because it overgrows native species (and can not be sold in nurseries in South Florida). Better for the West. Zone 9 and 10.

➤ *C. Cunninghamiana,* 60 to 70 feet. This variety is most hardy with dark green colored leaves. It has an upright habit of growth. Zone 9.

➤ *C. equisetifolia,* up to 60 feet. The name means leaves like the horsetail. The leaves are also dark green in color.

➤ *C. lepidophloia.* This tree suckers profusely and is not as salt tolerant as others. It sometimes has been grafted on the equisetifolia to help discontinue the suckering habit.

➤ *C. stricta.* This street tree should be watered until well established. Zone 10.

Catalpa speciosa
50 to 60 feet
This popular deciduous tree has huge leaves, sometimes a foot long. It is a rather large tree obtaining widths of 40 to 50 feet. The catalpa has white flowers with brown markings from late spring through summer followed by long, slender seed capsules. It is sometimes misnamed Indian bean, but the seed capsules are not to be eaten. This tree has good drought tolerance once established with some watering during the long, hot summer drought. Native plant. Zone 4.

Cedrus spp.
Cedar
60 to 70 feet
This attractive evergreen tree has short twigs with tufts of needles. Its cone is similar to that of the pine tree. This tree has a very deep root system and can survive even a hot summer with very little water once established. The male catkins do produce a lot of pollen. Zone 7.

➤ *C. atlantica,* Atlas Cedar, 60 feet. This slow-growing tree with angular growth habits can become a specimen tree when mature. It has blue-green, 1-inch, needlelike foliage. Some varieties are golden green, while others are bluish gray. Many of these trees have a weeping habit.

➤ *C. Deodara,* Deodar Cedar, 70 feet. The deodor cedar grows fast and can spread to one half of its height. There are some dwarf, prostrate, and golden varieties. The branches often sweep the ground. An outstanding specimen tree. This cedar takes pruning well in order to control its size.

➤ *C. libani,* Cedar of Lebanon, 70 feet. This irregular but attractive, slow-growing tree produces a lot of cones when young. It is gray-green in color.

Celtis spp.
Hackberry
20 to 50 feet
This deciduous tree looks similar to the elms, to which they are related. The birds feed on the tiny fruits. The hackberry takes many different soil types and withstands the summer heat. Ask your local nursery for the best hackberry for your region.

➤ *C. australis,* European Hackberry, 40 to 50 feet. This deciduous native of southern Europe has a moderate growth habit. Requires full sun. Zone 7.

➤ *C. laevigata,* Mississippi Hackberry (Sugarberry), 40 feet. The

Deodar Cedar.

Mississippi hackberry has a large, straight trunk with a rounded head that makes it an excellent specimen tree. Often grown for a naturalistic look in the landscape. Little care is required other than occasional waterings for it to look its best. Native to Illinois, South, and Texas. Zone 8.

➤ *C. occidentalis,* Common Hackberry, 50 feet. This tree with extremely wide leaves requires full sun. Native from Northeast to Southeast. Zone 7.

➤ *C. pallida,* Desert Hackberry, up to 20 feet. This is often shrublike and used in desert regions. The desert hackberry makes a nice hedge or screening plant.

➤ *C. reticulata,* Western Hackberry, 20 to 30 feet. This attractive ornamental tree is used in desert plantings. Native to Western plains and Southwest.

Ceratonia siliqua
St. John's Bread, Carob Tree
40 feet
This evergreen tree requires full sun. It is sometimes used as a multistemmed shrub, 15 to 20 feet. The female produces foot-long, flat, leathery, edible fruits. It also makes a good screening tree. Popular in Southern California and Arizona. Zone 9.

Cercidium floridum
Palo Verde
35 feet
This deciduous tree grows as wide as it grows tall. It has a showy, yellow flower followed by spine-filled, greenish blue leaves that fall in early winter. The palo verde grows well in desert conditions, and is native to the Southwest. Zone 7.

Cercis canadensis
Redbud
10 to 20 feet, sometimes taller
A small, deciduous, rounded ornamental tree with cheery red-pink blooms in early spring. Dark gray bark color. Native to East, down through Southeast and Texas. A good specimen planting, or combined with early-flowering shrubs and perennials. Tolerates many soils. Zone 5.

Cercis occidentalis
Western Redbud
10 to 20 feet
This deciduous tree or large shrub can have a single trunk but is often multi-trunked. It has 2- to 3-inch leaves and flowers in early spring, followed by red seed pods. Water well until established. The western red bud requires partial shade to near full sun. Native of California. Zone 7.

Chilopsis linearis
Desert Catalpa, Desert Willow
15 to 25 feet
This small tree or large shrub often has an irregular growth pattern. Many times

A Redbud (Cercis canadensis) *of the Southeast.*

William H. Allen, Jr.

the trunk is twisted but attractive. The leaves are 2 to 5 inches long and the flowers are white, pink, lavender, or burgundy with purple markings. These trumpet-shaped flowers are 2 inches long. The desert catalpa is native of Texas and the Southwest. Zone 7.

Chorisia speciosa
Floss Silk Tree
Up to 40 feet
This tree flowers in the fall with large red to pink flowers that are 6 to 7 inches across. The foliage drops in temperatures of 20°F. It requires good

drainage and full sun. Water the tree until established, then periodically during dry times. Zone 9–10.

Cinnamomum camphora
Camphor Tree
50 to 60 feet

This tree is known for its leaves: crush the camphor leaves to release the aroma. As a landscape tree, it is spreading with low branches that can reach 50 feet across. The camphor grows in most soils provided there is good drainage. Pruning is necessary to give the tree shape. Manganese deficiency on new growth may show up with alkaline soils. Zone 8.

Cornus florida
Flowering Dogwood
20 to 30 feet

Beautiful ornamental tree, with graceful, open canopy. In spring, the flowering dogwood is a mass of white (bracts, as opposed to flowers). Deciduous, with good red fall color. A native, from the Northeast to the Southeast, to eastern regions of Texas. Needs acidic soil. Zone 4.

Cupressocyparis leylandi
Leyland Cypress
50 feet

This tall, evergreen tree of pyramidal growth habit has arborvitaelike, fast growth. It is excellent for screening and requires full sun. Water well until established. Zone 6.

Cupressocyparis leylandi castlewellan
Castlewellan Cypress
50 feet

This dense evergreen tree of pyramidal form has new growth with golden color. It is a good screen plant and should be planted in full sun. Zone 6.

Cupressus spp.
Cypress
40 to 60 feet

➤ *C. arizonica,* Arizona Cypress (rough-barked, native to Southwest and Texas)
   C. glabra, Arizona Smooth-bark Cypress (native of Arizona)
   Both of these Southwestern trees shed their bark yearly, then show rich, cherry-red bark underneath.

Flowering Dogwood.

They have juniperlike foliage, gray-green to gray to gray-blue in color. These quick-growing trees take the heat and drought well. Require full sun. Zone 7.

➤ *C. sempervirens,* Italian cypress, up to 60 feet. This columnar, upright tree can be grown for screening or as a specimen tree. It requires full sun. Zone 7.

Dalbergia sissoo
Indian Rosewood
50 feet
Has an open growing habit. Often classified as a semi-evergreen, the Indian rosewood is tolerant of moist soils but can tolerate dry soils as well. It can be used as a framing or a background tree. Zone 9.

Elaeagnus spp.
5 to 20 feet
This evergreen or deciduous large shrub or small tree has many varieties. Many have a silvery coating of scales or pubescence on the leaves. The flowers are inconspicuous, small, about ¼ inch in size, and often fragrant. Most grow moderate to fast. Some varieties have a silvery or red fruit. It makes a good screening plant for privacy. Also good as a hedge plant. The elaeagnus grows well in many types of soils and prefers full sun. Water well to establish.

➤ *E. angustifolia,* Russian Olive, 20 feet. A deciduous tree with gray, silvery leaves 2 inches in size, giving it the olive tree look. With angular branches and fragrant, yellow-green flowers that are followed by small olivelike fruit. It takes extreme conditions of cold and heat. Water to establish. The angustifolia seems to grow better in colder, dryer conditions. Zone 3.

➤ *E. multiflora,* 6 to 8 feet. A deciduous small tree or large shrub has leaves that are silvery green on the topside and brown underneath. The tiny fragrant flowers are followed by reddish orange, ½-inch fruit that attracts birds. It requires full sun. Zone 7.

➤ *E. pungens,* Silverthorn, Silverberry. 5 to 15 feet. This small tree or large shrub has an irregular growth pattern that is often angular. It lends itself well to pruning. The Silverthorn, as the name suggests, has silvery gray-green foliage with a rust color on the twigs, giving a dull cast to the tree. The fruits are edible. A very tough plant that grows thick—a good screen plant. It is a bit gangly in its growth habit. Requires full sun. Zone 7.

Eriobotrya japonica
Loquat
15 to 35 feet
The Loquat tree has a spreading habit as it grows older and becomes full when planted in the sun, elongates when in shade. The large leaves are dark green in color, growing up to 12 inches. The

dull white flowers in the fall are followed by golden yellow, 2-inch-long fruit. Some varieties are tasty, with a nice mixture of acid and sweetness. It can be used as a specimen or background tree. Water well to establish and you must water often to get desired fruit. Plant in full sun to partial shade. Zone 8.

Eucalyptus spp.
Eucalyptus
40 to 100 feet
The majority of these evergreens are from Australia, New Zealand, and the islands nearby. There have been about 600 species described. Also commonly called gum tree in Australia. Water to establish, then you can forget to water, except during severe drought. They take the desert heat and Florida humidity. The eucalyptus are fast growers. Plant in a well-draining soil. Most varieties have inconspicuous white flowers.

➤ *E. camaldulensis,* Red Gum, 75 to 100 feet. This is a large spreading tree. Requires full sun. Zone 8.

➤ *E. citriodora,* Lemon-scented Gum, 75 to 100 feet. This upright growing tree with long leaves has a lemon scent. Zone 9.

➤ *E. Gunnii,* 40 to 80 feet. This large, full, upright tree requires full sun for best growth. Zone 8.

➤ *E. polyanthemos,* Silver-Dollar Eucalyptus, to 70 feet. in the West, to 30 or 40 feet in Florida. This

moderate to fast grower has silver-dollar-size leaves that are 2 to 3 inches across. The leaves become more elongated as the tree grows larger. Bigger in California and the West as it develops a deeper root system. Requires full sun. Zone 8.

There are many varieties to choose from, so check with your local nursery to see which one is best for your area.

Feijoa sellowiana
Pineapple Guava
15 to 28 feet
This evergreen tree or large shrub has dark, glossy green leaves on the top and white on the underside. It flowers from May through July with purple-white petals that have a mass of red stamens.

Pineapple Guava.

The edible fruit is gray-green in color and the bark is an attractive copper color. Requires full sun. Zone 8.

Ficus carica
Edible Fig
5 to 30 feet
This large shrub to medium-sized deciduous tree has a spreading growth habit when young. It has gray bark with dark green, 5- to 10-inch-wide leaves that are deeply lobed. The edible fig makes a nice specimen tree and grows well from California to Florida. Water to establish and plant in full sun. Three common varieties for the home garden are the 'Brown Turkey,' 'Celeste,' and 'Mission.' Zone 8.

Fraxinus spp.
Ash
30 to 45 feet
A deciduous tree, the ash is a moderate to fast grower. It has divided leaflets. The ash can be used as a specimen or street tree. Requires full sun.

➢ *F. modesto.* This variety has glossy green leaves that turn yellow in the fall.

➢ *F. pennsylvanica,* Green Ash, 30 to 45 feet. This moderate to fast grower can take drought or wet areas and extreme heat or cold. Native from Northeast to South. Zone 3.

➢ *F. velutina,* Arizona Ash, 30 to 50 feet. This native of southwestern United States can tolerate tough conditions.

Ginkgo biloba
Maidenhair Tree
30 to 50 feet
This deciduous tree has fan-shaped leaves that are 1 to 3 inches wide. The leaves turn a bright yellow before they drop in the fall. It has an irregular growth habit when young, becoming fuller when mature. This tree seems to withstand pollution well.

Grevillea spp.
75 feet
Large group of evergreen trees and shrubs from Australia with many new species and hybrids being developed. Water well to establish and then only during severe droughts. In alkaline soils Grevillea may show iron chlorosis.

➢ *G. robusta,* Silk Oak Tree, 50 to 75 feet. This fast-growing, large tree with leaves that grow 4 to 6 inches long has showy golden orange flowers in the spring. The younger trees are symmetrical, but as they age or get topped-off, they develop spreading habits. This tree drops more leaves than some people like. In Florida and other lightning-prone states, the silk oak makes an excellent lightening rod.

➢ *G. 'Noellii.'* This small tree or large shrub has horizontal branches and 1- to 2-inch needlelike leaves. This plant grows 4 to 6 feet wide and is a good hedge choice. It has pink and white cluster flowers in the spring. It does poorly in Florida. Zone 9.

Gymnocladus dioica
Coffee Tree
50 to 100 feet
This tree has leaflets on 12- to 30-inch leaves with dark green foliage that turns yellow in the fall. Its inconspicuous flowers (female flowers have 12-inch pink racemes) are preceded by reddish brown pods that carry hard black seeds. In times past, these seeds were roasted as a coffee substitute. This tree requires full sun. Native to East and upper Southeast. Zone 7.

Hakea spp.
Pincushion Tree
10 to 30 feet
This small, evergreen tree or large shrub from Australia takes high winds well and is heat tolerant. It is also tolerant of most soils that have good drainage. It requires full sun for best growth. Zone 9.

➤ *H. laurina,* Sea Urchin Tree, 10 to 30 feet. This small tree or large shrub has gray-green leaves and red to crimson, pincushionlike flowers.

➤ *H. suaveolens,* Sweet Hakea, 10 to 20 feet. This tree has deep green leaves that are 3 to 4 inches long and divided into segments. It makes an excellent screening tree.

➤ *H. victoria,* Royal Hakea, 6 to 10 feet. This small tree to narrow shrub

has broad, cupped leaves that are leathery and may be marked with colors of yellow and orange.

Ilex decidua
Possumhaw Holly
12 to 15 feet
Outstanding small deciduous ornamental tree: it has a profuse and brilliant orange-red berry display on bare branches in winter through spring. Multitrunked with pale gray bark. Buy female plants in berry, with a male nearby. Sun to partial shade. This is a native tree, from the eastern portions of the Midwest to the Southeast, down to Texas and Florida. Zone 5.

Ilex opaca
American Holly
40 to 50 feet
A dense, upright, pyramidal evergreen tree that is popular all over the United States. It is a native, from the lower Northeastern, Southern, and Southeastern woods. It has male and female flowers on different trees, so select female plants in berry. The fruit adds much to the holiday season and pleases the birds as well. Mulching is recommended to help retain moisture. The American holly is tolerant of many soils. Zone 6.

Ilex vomitoria
Yaupon Holly
12 to 15 feet
Attractive evergreen ornamental tree or large shrub, with a spread almost as

wide as the tree is tall. Multitrunked with olive-gray bark. Winter berries are small and vivid red, glossy; some varieties have yellow berries. As with the American holly, buy female plants in fruit to be sure of berries, and be sure a male holly is nearby. Native from the Southeast through Texas. Zone 7.

Jacaranda mimosifolia
30 to 50 feet
This deciduous to semi-evergreen tree, depending on the winter weather, is often multitrunked. The leaves are feathery and fernlike. New growth appears in the spring after the mature growth has fallen. The trumpet-shaped flowers are showy clusters of lavender blue. The jacaranda tolerates severe droughts when watered. The young trees may get injured in temperatures of mid-20°F. This tree requires full sun. Zone 9.

Juglans spp.
Walnut
15 to 150 feet
This deciduous tree has featherlike, divided leaves. The nuts have hard shells.

➤ *J. californica,* California Walnut, 15 to 30 feet. This native to southern California is a small tree.

➤ *J. hindsii,* California Black Walnut, 40 to 60 feet. The California walnut has fruit that is ¾ inch in diameter. Often used as a street or avenue planting. It has been used as a breeding stock for English walnuts.

This tree is native to northern California.

➤ *J. major,* Arizona Walnut, to 50 feet. The Arizona walnut grows from Arizona to New Mexico. It has excellent drought tolerance. Zone 7.

Juniperus silicicola
Southern Red Cedar
50 feet
When young, this tree is cone-shaped, becoming more open upon maturity. With small, scalelike, dark green leaves, the southern red cedar is much like other juniper members. This tree is often used as a screening or background tree, or as a Christmas tree when young. It is also used as a framing element in the landscape since it can reach 30 feet across. Native to Southeast and Florida. Zone 7.

Koelreuteria formosana
Golden Raintree
25 to 40 feet
This deciduous tree has a moderate growth rate with an open habit for good shade. The leaves are divided into 1- to 2-inch, toothed leaflets. The golden raintree has bright flowers in the fall, followed by pink, papery seed capsules that are more noticeable than the flowers. Most people assume they are the flowers. Water well to first establish, then only in drought conditions. This tree can be planted in partial shade to full sun. Zone 7.

Lagerstroemia indica
Crape Myrtle
5 to 25 feet
This small to medium-sized tree, which can also be a large shrub, clusters with frothy blooms that are almost paperlike in June through September. The colors include red, lavender, purple, and white. The crape myrtle is also noted for its smooth, gray-to-light-brown bark. The leaves turn color after the first frost. Frost damage is a common problem, but some new varieties are frost resistant. There are many named varie- ties. Be sure to look for powdery- mil- dew-resistant ones. The crape myrtle requires full sun and should be watered well to establish, with pruning during the dormant season. Zone 7.

Laurus nobilis
Sweet Bay
Up to 40 feet
This single or multitrunked tree to large shrub makes a good hedge or screening plant. The 3- to 4-inch leaves are used in cooking. It has small, yellow flowers with clusters of black berries that follow.

Sweet Gum.

Scott Ogden

Ligustrum japonicum
Japanese Privet
10 to 15 feet

This small tree or large, spreading, evergreen shrub can be used as a screening tree or as a hedge. When kept trimmed up, it makes an excellent tree or topiary. Water well to first establish, then only during severe droughts. The privet requires full sun to partial shade. Zone 7.

Liquidambar styraciflua
Sweet Gum
Up to 50 feet

This deciduous tree needs to be watered when first being established, then only during droughts. It has a narrow growth habit. Many people confuse this tree with the maple because the leaves are similar. The sweet gum provides great fall color even in mild winter areas. It requires full sun. Native plant, from the Northeast to the Southeast and Florida. Zone 5.

Magnolia grandiflora
Southern Magnolia
60 to 80 feet

A popular tree throughout the South. Not a true, drought-tolerant tree in all parts of the country, but once established, the southern magnolia has survived in Florida without extra irrigation other than rains. It is an evergreen tree that has a symmetric pyramidal form and large white, fragrant flowers. The southern magnolia requires full sun. Native of the Southeast over to Texas. Zone 6.

Bloom of the Southern Magnolia.

Walter K. Taylor

Myrica cerifera
Wax Myrtle
20 feet

Evergreen, small tree, native to the
eastern United States, the Southeast
over to Texas. Multitrunked, with grey
bark. Has blue berries that attract birds.
Water well at first to establish. Zone 7.

Olea europaea
Common Olive Tree
20 to 30 feet

This slow- to moderate-growing, evergreen tree has been described since
ancient times. It has willowlike leaves
that are gray-green and silver. The olive
tree's fruit is edible only when processed. This tree seems to prefer the
Rocky Mountain-type soil and conditions, but has acclimated to many
warmer areas of the United States.
Zone 8.

Wax Myrtle.

WATER-THRIFTY PALMS

Arecastrum Romanzoffianum
Queen Palm
40 feet

The queen palm, with a smooth gray-
brown trunk, is often planted as a
single-trunked specimen, but is sometimes effectively grouped in two's or
three's. Also used as an avenue palm.
Once established, it is water-thrifty.
Note: Make sure to fertilize with extra
manganese and magnesium. Zone 9.

Butia capitata
Pindo Palm
20 feet

This single-trunked palm has a gray-
brown trunk, 2 feet in diameter, with
blue-green, graceful fronds that can
reach 6 feet in length. It makes an excellent street tree or specimen in the
landscape. Zone 9.

Caryota mitis
Fishtail Palm
25 to 30 feet

Multi-trunked; slender trunks (4 to 5 inches in diameter). The leaflets are light green and somewhat resemble fishtails. The fishtail palm is sometimes grown in large pots or containers for the deck or patio, but it is occasionally used as a specimen or avenue palm. Fairly water tolerant once established. Note: After each trunk is through with flowering and fruiting, it will die (similar to what happens with a banana tree). Therefore, the trunk needs to be removed. Zone 9.

Chamaerops humilis
European Fan Palm
5 to 15 feet

Single or multi-trunked; trunks can reach 1 foot in diameter. The leaf color is dark gray-green. It is often used as a specimen or in planter boxes—any-

European Fan Palm.

where a slow-growing palm is desired. Sun to partial shade; mediterranean plant. Zone 9.

Phoenix canariensis
Canary Island Date Palm
50 feet

A large, straight, single-trunked palm, sometimes called the pineapple palm. The trunk can reach 2 to 4 feet in diameter. As with most palms, it requires extra manganese and magnesium in addition to a regular fertilizer. Improve the soil at planting time and water frequently to establish—once it is established, the Canary Island date palm is drought-tolerant. Zone 9.

Phoenix reclinata
Senegal Date Palm
40 feet

A multitrunked *Phoenix* member. Most trunks are 6 to 9 inches in diameter. You'll often see this clump palm used as a specimen in both commercial and residential landscapes. It grows more quickly than some palms. Although most landscapers improve the soil when planting, it grows best in well-draining soil. Zone 9.

Sabal Palmetto
Cabbage Palm
75 feet

Tall, straight, single-trunked palm often used as a background or avenue planting, sometimes as a specimen. The bark becomes gray as it ages. This is the official state tree of Florida, and is therefore protected. It has excellent salt tolerance. Native to Florida and the Carolinas. Zone 8.

Coontie.

Washingtonia robusta
Washington Palm
80 feet
Slender, single, straight palm from Mexico whose trunk rises from a larger base and ends with palmate leaves that can be 4 to 5 feet wide. Old fronds droop and hang, giving the palm a "petticoat" effect if the fronds are not removed. Tolerant of almost any soil, the Washington palm can be almost forgotten once established. Zone 9.

Zamia floridana
Coontie
Shrublike Florida native with attractive, divided fronds that almost hide a short trunk. Integrates well in a garden design or as a specimen planting. Zone 9.

Parkinsonia aculeata
Jerusalem Thorn
20 to 40 feet
A deciduous tree with an upright and open growth habit. It has an interesting shape with bark that is lime green in color. The leaves fall with the first frost or severe droughts; they are 5 to 8 inches long with small leaflets. In the spring, the pea-shaped, yellow flowers have a pleasant fragrance. It tolerates a high pH range and can be used from desert to ocean sites. It requires full sun. Zone 7.

Pinus spp.
Pine
20 to 100 feet
These are evergreen trees with needles that are produced in bundles. These pines require good drainage and tolerate most soils. There is a good pine variety for every part of the country.

➢ *P. canariensis,* Canary Island Pine, up to 80 feet. This fast-growing, evergreen tree has a rounded head. It has 8-inch oval cones and a general graceful appearance. It requires full sun. Zone 8.

Jerusalem Thorn.

Scott Ogden

> *P. clausa,* Sand Pine, up to 50 feet. As the name implies, this tree is great in sandy soils. It requires full sun.

> *P. elliotti,* Slash Pine. This upright tree with needlelike leaves has a strong central leader. Native of the Southeast. Zone 8.

> *P. eldarica,* Eldarica Pine, 50 to 60 feet. This evergreen tree has a pyramidal growth habit. It is tolerant of the California coastal winds, along with drought and desert-type conditions. It requires full sun. Zone 6.

> *P. halepensis,* Aleppo Pine, up to 50 feet. This fast-growing evergreen has a large spreading crown and is also tolerant of coastal and desert conditions. Zone 8.

> *P. palustris,* Longleaf Pine, up to 90 feet. A native to the Southeast: Florida, Georgia, Virginia, Alabama, and Mississippi. Prefers sandy soils. Zone 7.

Longleaf Pine.

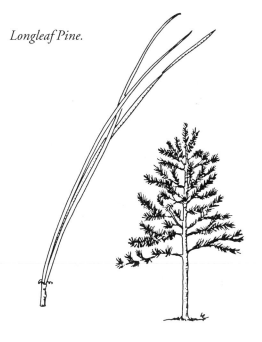

➤ *P. radiata,* Monterey Pine, 50 to 80 feet. This moderate- to fast-growing California native has a symmetrical shape. It holds cones a long time. It will take the California coastal conditions and requires full sun. Zone 7.

➤ *P. roxburghii,* Chir Pine, 60 to 80 feet. This pyramidal-growing, evergreen tree becomes symmetrical when mature. It tolerates coastal conditions. Zone 6.

➤ *P. thunbergiana, P. thunbergii,* Japanese Black Pine, up to 100 feet. Although this broadly, pyramidal evergreen can grow up to 100 feet in California, it stays much smaller when grown in Florida, 20 to 30 feet (where it would make an excellent Bonsai subject). The Japanese black pine requires full sun. Zone 6.

Pistacia chinensis
Chinese Pistache
40 to 60 feet
This deciduous tree is a slow to moderate grower. It has an irregular growth habit when young. The leaves are 2 to 4 inches with the color of red-scarlet to yellow-orange in the fall. It requires a high pH range and tolerates drought, but should be watered during summer droughts. Full sun is also required. Zone 7.

Prosopis spp.
Mesquite
10 to 30 feet
These evergreen or deciduous trees with spreading branches have small flowers followed by spikes with flat seed pods. The mesquite tree grows best in Texas, Arizona, and parts of California. It does take the heat well and tolerates

Mesquite.

William D. Adams

droughts. The mesquite prefers high pH range. Although this tree might be thought of as a western-grown tree, some grown in Florida are doing well in parking lots and other sandy areas.

➤ *P. alba,* Argentine Mesquite. This single-trunked, fast- growing tree has black-green leaves on a thick canopy.

➤ *P. chilensis,* Chilean Mesquite. There may be hybrids of this deciduous tree. It has deep green foliage.

➤ *P. glandulosa,* Texas Mesquite. This deciduous tree has dark green leaves and drooping branches. Native of Oklahoma and Texas. One variety, *P. glandulosa Torreyana,* is a native of the Southwest and Southern California.

➤ *P. velutina,* Arizona Mesquite. This Arizona native is more often used as a shrub than most other varieties.

Prunus spp.
10 to 40 feet
These deciduous or evergreen trees and shrubs include the peach, plum, and other ornamental varieties.

➤ *P. caroliniana,* Cherry Laurel, 30 to 40 feet. This plant can be trimmed as a hedge or as a screening tree. It has dark green foliage with 2- to-4-inch long leaves, with small white flowers that are followed by ¼- to ½-inch black fruits. The cherry laurel takes heat, wind, and almost any soil type. Requires full

Sun. Native of the Southeast to Texas. Zone 7.

➤ *P. cistena,* Dwarf Red Leaf Plum, 6 to 10 feet. This deciduous tree or large shrub has dark red to purple leaves with white to pink flowers and dark purple fruit. Zone 3.

➤ *P. ilicifolia,* Holly-leaf Cherry, 20 to 35 feet. This evergreen, small tree has dark green holly type (spiny) leaves. It flowers in the spring with 6-inch spikes and purple-red fruit that are ¾ to 1 inch in size. This fruit can be eaten but it is mostly pit. Water well when first establishing. The holly-leaf cherry prefers good drainage and full sun to partial shade. Native of Baja California. Zone 7.

Punica granatum
Pomegranate
40 to 80 feet
This deciduous, small tree or large shrub is sometimes single trunked but often is seen with many trunks that branch low. It has slender green leaves that turn vivid yellow-orange in the fall. The pomegranate produces reddish orange flowers in the late spring to early summer, which become deep red fruits in fall and early winter. This tree tolerates drought but should be watered for best fruit production. Some dwarf varieties may require more water. It tolerates a high pH range and prefers full sun. Zone 8.

Quercus spp.
Oak

Some are evergreen trees while others are considered deciduous trees. Most oaks have good drought tolerance once you get them established. Be careful not to change the grade of the soil if you are lucky enough to have them on your existing property.

➤ *Q. agrifolia,* Coast Live Oak of California, 40 to 75 feet. This native of California has an open, spreading habit of growth. It is an evergreen tree with a large, rounded canopy. The leaves are hollylike and are dropped in the spring just before new leaves come on. It requires full sun. Zone 7.

➤ *Q. Ilex,* Holly Oak, 50 to 70 feet. This native of the Mediterranean has been used in California. Its heavy foliage can sometimes be sheared into topiary shapes. The holly oak's leaves are 2 to 4 inches long. It requires full sun. Zone 7.

➤ *Q. macrocarpa,* Bur Oak, 50 to 75 feet. This oak is native to the Midwest, Northeast, Southeast, and Texas. Its spread is often greater than its height. The round leaves are 6 to 10 inches long. This tree is cold hardy. It requires full sun. Zone 4.

➤ *Q. palustris,* Pin Oak, 50 to 80 feet. This deciduous tree droops its lower branches but has a pyramidal habit of growth. The scarlet color of the leaves in fall signals the coming of winter. It requires full sun. Native from Northeast to Southeast. Zone 4.

➤ *Q. Shumardii,* Shumard Red Oak, 60 feet. Good shade tree, native to the Southeast through to Texas. Rounded shape, deciduous, with vivid red fall color. Leaves to 5 inches. Zone 5.

➤ *Q. stellata,* Post Oak, 50 to 60 feet. Native oak from Northeast (Massachusetts) to South. T-shaped, lobed leaves. If post oaks exist on property, try to keep from disturbing the area around them.

➤ *Q. suber,* Cork Oak, up to 60 feet. This tree spreads almost the same as its height and can be seen growing in California. It obtained its name from the bark, which is sold as cork. The cork oak is very drought tolerant after watering well to establish. It requires full sun. Zone 7.

➤ *Q. virginiana,* Live Oak, 50 to 70 feet. This evergreen has dark green, cupped leaves with an overall wide, spreading habit of growth. It is the aristocrat of trees and has long been used as an avenue planting. The majesty of this tree belongs to the equally spreading, long, impressive branches and trunks. The live oak lives for centuries. It is tolerant of salt and desert conditions. Requires full sun. Native of the Southeast and Florida. Zone 7.

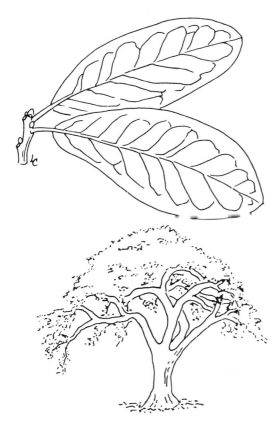

Live Oak.

Rhus spp.
Sumac
8 to 30 feet

This whole group is tolerant of poor soils and droughts. They consist of evergreen trees and deciduous ones. Good drainage is a must. Many native American species.

➤ *R. glabra,* up to 20 feet. This small tree has 2- to 5-inch long leaves that are narrow and fernlike. They turn vivid scarlet colors in the fall. Native to Plains, Rockies, and Southwest.

➤ *R. ovata,* Sugarbush, up to 10 feet. This shrub to small tree has long glossy leaves, red fruit, and white-pink flowers. Native to Southwest; good for desert conditions.

Robinia spp.
Locust
10 to 50 feet

These deciduous trees or shrubs are tolerant of droughts, heat, and cold. The flowers are pea-shaped and hang between divided leaflets. They do have brittle wood and may sucker. Native American tree, in many regions.

Sambucus canadensis 'Aurea'
American Elderberry
6 to 10 feet

This deciduous small tree or large shrub has flat, white flower clusters followed by edible fruit. This fruit is used for wines and pies. It requires full sun. Native to eastern half of United States. Zone 4.

Sapium sebiferum
Chinese Tallow Tree
30 to 40 feet

This deciduous tree has spread equal to its height. Produces fall color of golden to red leaves. It makes an excellent screening plant. Requires full sun. Zone 8.

Schinus molle
California Pepper Tree
20 to 40 feet
The width of this tree equals that of its height. The California pepper tree has bright green leaves that are aromatic leaflets on pendulous branches. Yellow flowers are followed by red berries. It requires full sun. Despite the name, not a California native. Zone 9.

Schinus terebinthifolius
Brazilian Pepper Tree
20 to 40 feet
This small- to medium-sized tree is quite drought tolerant. It is considered a "weed" tree in Florida because it will take over the native species (and is not sold in South Florida nurseries). It has white or yellow flowers followed by bright red berries. It requires full sun. Zone 9.

Tabebuia **spp.**
Trumpet Tree
20 to 25 feet
There are about 100 species of Tabebuia. Some have pink, white, and yellow flowers. Most of these trees have irregular, spreading limbs, which make it a nice street tree in the warmer areas. It will tolerate many soils and requires full sun. Zone 9-10.

➤ *T. argentea,* Silver Trumpet Tree, 20 to 25 feet. This deciduous tree has an open, yet irregular, growth habit. It has light gray, corky bark and silvery gray leaves. The beautiful silver-gray, trumpet-shaped flowers bring a nice fragrance in the spring before the new leaves appear. Protected areas of Zone 9.

➤ *T. pallida,* Pink Trumpet, 25 feet. A small, slender-trunked tree with scaly bark. It is semi-evergreen depending on winter temperatures. A nice specimen or avenue tree. The pink, trumpet-shaped blooms are up to 3 inches in length. Good drought tolerance. Protected areas of Zone 9.

DROUGHT-TOLERANT SHRUBS

Shrubs bring unity to the landscape. They help tie the landscape design together. Not only do shrubs soften lines but they also often add visual focal points in the landscape. Usually under ten feet tall, most shrubs will have more than one stem, although some shrubs can be grown as standards or as small treelike plants. Shrubs will often vary in their growth habits and in size. Their leaves can vary from tiny, to needlelike, to large (2 feet or more across). Some shrubs are grown for their flowers, others for their shape, berry or fruit, still others for their interesting texture or color.

You'll often see shrubs used in border plantings—at the border of a landscape feature or at the edge of the lawn where it meets the neighbor's yard or the street. Shrub borders create separate areas in the landscape.

The following choices of shrubs should help you with success in your quest for a beautiful garden. If a shrub doesn't thrive, it may be that the light, temperature, or ability to withstand dry conditions wasn't correct.

Abelia × *grandiflora*
Glossy Abelia
Up to 8 feet, 7 feet in mild climates
This evergreen shrub has fragrant, white flowers. It is tolerant of many different soil types and takes partial shade to full sun. The abelia makes an excellent specimen planting or an attractive hedge. Zone 6.

Abelia grandiflora × *schumannii*
Edward Goucher
3 feet in mild climates
This dwarf form abelia makes a great informal hedge plant. It is an evergreen that has small lavender-pink flowers. The abelia likes partial shade to full sun. Zone 6.

A hot color combination: brilliant Red Oleander in the background with Pavonia in the foreground.

William D. Adams

Aesculus californica
California Buckeye
10 to 15 feet

This large shrub can also be trimmed as a small tree. It has cream-colored flowers that are upright on the tips of the branches in the spring, followed by long seed capsules that open to show bright, shiny, inedible nuts. The California Buckeye may drop its foliage during hot, dry summers, but survives drought. It requires full sun. California native. Zone 7.

Agave spp.
Agave
1 to 6 feet

Desert conditions come to mind when talking about this plant. Agave grows well from California, Arizona, Texas, and Florida where the temperatures do not go below mid-teens. A succulent, it has stiff, thick, spine-tipped leaves.

➤ *A. americana,* Century Plant, 3 to 6 feet. This plant is called the century plant because most people thought it produced a flower stalk every 100 years, but it really occurs in 8 to 12 years. The century plant makes an impressive feature in a landscape, with its long swordlike leaves with spines that look like needles. These are dark blue-green leaves sometimes striped with white or yellow. This plant has a poisonous sap. After flowering, the main plant needs to be taken out. Small plants will grow up near the old base. There are many varieties of the century plant to choose from. It requires full sun to partial shade. Native to Southwest. Zone 8.

Alyogyne huegelii
Blue Hibiscus
4 to 8 feet
This evergreen shrub has rough-textured foliage and lilac-blue flowers 4 to 6 inches across. It blooms most of the year. Plant in a protected area when temperatures reach mid 20s. Requires full sun. Zone 9.

Aralia balfouriana
(Polyscias Balfouriana)
5 to 20 feet
The evergreen leaves of Aralia are rounded and 3 to 4 inches wide. Most varieties have leaves that are splotched with white. This upright, narrow hedge plant can be used in tropical areas with its requirement of full sun to partial shade.

➤ *Dizgotheca kerchoveana,* False Aralia, 5 to 15 feet. The leaves on this plant resemble a human hand. The finely cut, dark green leaves can be 8 to 12 inches long and 5 to 10 inches wide. It makes a great tropical effect. The false aralia is often used as a specimen in frost-free areas of the United States. It is tolerant of many different soil types and requires full sun to partial shade. Zone 9.

Arctostaphylos manzanita
Manzanita
This evergreen shrub (also a creeping groundcover) can be trimmed up to a small tree in size. Most have leatherlike foliage with interesting branches that sprout white or pink blossoms. This plant requires good drainage and is moderately drought tolerant once established. It does best in California (native) as well as the West and Northwest. Zone 5–7.

➤ *A.* × 'Jade Spreader' *manzanita,* 10 to 12 inches. Too much water can kill this plant. It requires full sun and has great drought tolerance. This evergreen groundcover has dark green foliage complemented by red stems and pink blossoms. Zone 7.

➤ *A. Uva-ursi* 'Point Reyes Kinnikinick.' This evergreen groundcover is one foot tall and has a 15-inch spread with pink blossoms. Good red fall color. The kinnikinick takes heat, smog, and drought well.

Artemisia **spp.**
Artemisia
2 to 4 feet
These shrubs or low-growing perennials have inconspicuous flowers, but their attraction is their handsome silver-gray foliage. Some species are herbs. They like an improved, organic soil with good drainage. Mostly in the West. Artemisia are tolerant to both cold and drought.

➤ *A. absinthium,* Common Wormwood, 2 to 4 feet. A perennial evergreen with feathery, silver-gray leaves and insignificant yellow flowers.

➤ *A. caucasica* 'Silver Spreader,' 3 to 8 inches. This shrub has silvery, finely cut leaves with inconspicuous yellow flowers.

➤ *A. ludoviciana,* Silver King, 3 to 4 feet. Very hardy—can take the heat. Plant in full sun in well-draining soil. Can be invasive, so use a border or edge to keep it contained. Native in South, Southwest, on up to Northwest and Plains.

➤ *A. Schmidtiana,* Silver Mound or Angel's Hair. This low-growing perennial with silver-gray, fernlike foliage is excellent in rock gardens or as a border plant. It prefers full sun. Zone 2.

➤ *A. Stellerana* 'Silver Brocade,' 4 to 5 inches. This shrub has a nice habit of growth with woody stems at the base but herbaceous tips. It also has felt-like, white leaves and requires full sun. Zone 3.

Asclepias tuberosa
Butterfly Weed
2 to 5 feet
A perennial plant that sends up 2- to 3-foot stems topped with bright orange and yellow flowers. It requires full sun and water during the heat of summer. As its name implies, it attracts butterflies. Native to East and Southeast of United States. Zone 8.

Aspidistra elatior
Cast-Iron Plant
Up to 24 inches
A super houseplant for dark areas, outside, this evergreen perennial tolerates neglect if in protected areas in Florida and the Coastal South. It is sometimes called the spittoon plant from the Old West Days. It has long, linear leaves. Zone 7.

Atriplex **spp.**
Saltbush
1 to 4 feet
This evergreen, sometimes deciduous shrub is great for ocean-side plantings because it tolerates salt and a high pH soil range, as well as droughts. It has gray-silver leaves, and birds are attracted to the flowers and the fruit.

➤ *A. canescens,* Four-wing Saltbush, 2 to 6 feet. This evergreen has ½- to 2-inch-long slender, gray leaves. It

Butterfly Weed.

Walter K. Taylor

tolerates temperatures below 0°F. Native to Northwest, West, Plains, and Texas.

➤ *A. lentiformis,* Quail Bush, 3 to 10 feet. This shrub can get 10 to 12 feet wide. It has blue-gray leaves that are 1 to 2 inches long (many varieties are full of spines). The quail bush makes an excellent hedge plant. It takes desert soils and a high pH range. Native to Southwest deserts.

➤ *A. semibaccata,* Australian Saltbush. This small shrub, growing to about 1 foot tall and 6 inches wide, is excellent for holding the soil together. Requires full sun. Zone 8.

Aucuba japonica
Japanese Aucuba
5 to 10 feet
The leathery leaves of this aucuba grow 4 to 8 inches long and most varieties have dark green leaves, while other leaves are variegated. It has inconspicuous flowers with red berries. The Japanese aucuba has fair drought tolerance but is attractive enough to consider planting in protected areas. It does require filtered sunlight to deep shade. Zone 7.

➤ *Aucuba japonica* 'Picturata,' Gold Spot Aucuba, up to 6 feet. This evergreen shrub has glossy green leaves with gold centers. It requires

filtered sunlight to deep shade.
Zone 7.

➤ *Aucuba japonica* 'Variegata,' Gold
Dust Plant, up to 6 feet. An evergreen shrub with dotted foliage of
gold variegation. It likes filtered sun
to shade. Zone 7.

Baccharis pilularis
Coyote Bush
1 to 2 feet
An evergreen, low-growing shrub that
can spread 4 to 6 feet. Makes an excellent groundcover, but its flowers are
insignificant. Cuttings from the male
plant are recommended. A California
native of coastal areas. It is unsurpassed
for desert, oceanside, and dune areas,
and tolerates both dry conditions and
rain. Zone 9

Beaucarnea recurvata
Ponytail Palm
Up to 15 feet
This large shrub or small tree with a
greatly swollen base or trunk has recurv-
ing, grasslike, narrow leaves. This plant
is often used as a houseplant or a conver-
sation piece. Once established, you need
only to water during the dry periods. It
requires full sun to partial shade.
Zone 9.

Berberis spp.
Barberry
5 to 6 feet

➤ *B. gladwynensis* 'William Penn,' 5
feet. An evergreen shrub that grows

to be a vigorous hedge or barrier
shrub. It has bright yellow flowers
and needs to be planted in full sun.
Zone 6.

➤ *B.* × *mentorensis,* Mentor Barberry,
up to 6 feet. This deciduous shrub
has yellow flowers followed by red
berries and a beautiful red fall color.
Very drought tolerant. It requires full
sun. Zone 4.

➤ *B. thunbergii* 'Atropurpurea,' Red
Leaf Barberry, 5 to 6 feet. This
deciduous barberry is dense with red
foliage and small yellow flowers. It
requires full sun. Zone 4.

➤ *B. thunbergii* 'Aurea,' Yellow Leaf
Barberry, 3 to 4 feet. A deciduous
shrub with golden yellow foliage that
makes an excellent specimen plant. It
requires full sun to partial shade.
Zone 5.

➤ *B. thunbergii* 'Crimson Pygmy,' 1 to
2 feet. The Crimson Pygmy makes
an excellent foundation plant with
its blood red foliage. It is a deciduous
shrub that requires full sun. Zone 4.

➤ *B. thunbergii* 'Rose Glow,' 5 to 6
feet. This deciduous shrub has
variegated pink new growth
becoming rose-red upon maturity.
It requires full sun to partial shade.
Zone 4.

➤ *B. trifoliata (Mahonia trifoliata),*
Agarita, to 6 feet. Good barrier shrub
of dark foliage. Texas native, for
Texas and Southwest.

Agarita (Berberis rrifoliata).

William D. Adams

Bougainvillea spp.
Bougainvillea
Variable

Bougainvillea.

Some varieties of this vigorous, large evergreen have a shrublike growth pattern, while other varieties have a vining growth habit and should be planted in the warmer areas of the United States. Protect bougainvilleas from freezing weather. Water well until established, then it can tolerate droughts well. The bracts (flowers) come in many colors—red, purple, pink, orange, yellow, or white. Some bracts change as they get older. Be sure not to over-fertilize or trim excessively if mass blossoms are the desired effect you choose. Fertilize with a food that is lower in nitrogen, higher in phosphorus and potassium. Requires full sun. Native of South America. Zone 9-10.

Walter K. Taylor

BOUGAINVILLEA

Variety	Color
Barbara Karst	brilliant crimson red
Betty Hendry	true red
California Gold	golden orange
Coral	striking orange and pink
Double Orange	good orange color with double flowers
Double Pink	orchid pink, double flowers
Double White	white with pink-blush
Glabra	large cluster of purple
James Walker	light orange changing to pink, then lavender
La Jolla	fluorescent red, bush form used in hanging baskets

Variety	Color
Lavender Queen	pale lilac, lavender
Mary Palmer's Enchantment	pure white
Orange King	sunset rose to yellow-orange
Raspberry Ice	bright magenta, variegated foliage with pale yellow margins, bush form to 3 feet, sometimes used in hanging baskets
Royal Purple	deep, rich purple
San Diego Red	dark red
Southern Rose	phlox pink
Temple Fire	bronze-red, bush form mounding to 24 feet, fantastic groundcover
White Madonna	white with pink blush

Buxus microphylla japonica
Japanese Boxwood
5 to 6 feet

A slow-growing shrub with opposite leaves. This plant is sometimes kept in containers or used as a sheared hedge planting. It requires full sun to partial shade. Japanese boxwood is prone to nematode problems in the South. Zone 7.

➤ 'Green Beauty,' up to 6 feet. This is used for a hedge plant or a sheared specimen. Requires full sun to partial shade. Zone 5.

➤ 'Winter Gem,' up to 6 feet. This evergreen shrub is used as a clipped hedge or border planting. A hardy variety that holds green color through the winter. It requires full sun to partial shade. Zone 5.

Cactacae
Cactus Family
Variable

Cactus is a very large family of plants. We tend to think of desert conditions or the Old Wild, Wild West when we think of cacti, which is valid thinking considering that many members of this family grow in just these types of settings. Most cacti prefer being planted in full sun and many like the warm temperatures of the day and can tolerate the lower temperatures of 40°F at night. Some members can even tolerate a light frost. Many will go dormant in the winter. A sandy soil is best for good growth.

➤ *Cacti* spp. These are some of the most drought tolerant plants we have. Almost all of them are native to the Americas. Even without water, the cacti will live, although they may not grow under these conditions. Cacti do grow in many shapes, from buttonlike peyote to upright cacti such as the barrel cacti and the spectacular saguaro, *Cereus giganteus* or *Carnegiea gigantea*. Cacti have adapted to dry environment areas because of features such as thick stems that retain water, an extensive root system, and a lack of leaves on the majority of the group. It is estimated that there are up to 1,500 different species.

➤ *Cereus peruvianus,* Hedge Cactus, Peruvian Apple Cactus. A fast growing, upright, columnlike growth, this native of South America makes a spectacular specimen in the landscape. It has blue-green stems with beautiful, white, night-blooming, 2- to 12-inch flowers. The height of the hedge cactus could be 20 to 25 feet tall. The hedge cactus likes a well-draining soil and full sun to partial shade. Zone 9.

Caesalpinia pulcherrima
Dwarf Poinciana, Barbados Pride
10 to 15 feet
A fast-growing, large, deciduous shrub with flowers of orange-red—showy clusters of good quality. It tolerates many soils, even desert conditions, and requires full sun. Zone 9.

Barbados Pride.

Scott Ogden

Calliandra spp.
Powder Puff
15 feet
This plant has sprawling, evergreen foliage that is compound. The powder puff flowers consist mostly of stamens.

➤ *C. eriophylla,* Fairy Duster, 3 to 4 feet. This open shrub is 4 to 5 feet wide with clusters of pink to red flowers in 2-inch powder puffs in early spring. Cold hardy, to 0°F. Requires full sun. Southwest native. Zone 7.

➤ *C. haematocephala,* up to 15 feet. A shrub that sprawls all over to make huge mounds of powder-puff flowers of red, pink, or white. It requires full sun and can be watered on rare occasions once established. Zone 9.

➤ *C. Tweedii,* Trinidad Flame Bush, 5 to 8 feet. This tall shrub has an open habit of growth. Flowers are bright red. The Trinidad flame bush requires full sun. Zone 9.

Callicarpa japonica
Japanese Beautyberry
4 to 6 feet
A deciduous shrub as wide as it is tall. The flowers are light pink with deep purple berries that seem metallic. It requires full sun to partial shade. Zone 5.

Caragana
Pea Shrub
10 to 20 feet
This shrub to small tree originates from Siberia, Russia. It has small leaflets with small yellow flowers. Naturally it can tolerate the cold of the United States— in cold desert regions and in the Northwest. Zone 3.

Carissa grandiflora
Natal Plum
5 to 10 feet
An evergreen shrub with dark green, oval, shiny, 2-inch leaves. It has white,

starlike, fragrant flowers that are followed by purple-red fruit. Most of these have spines on branches with a 5- to 8-foot spread. The natal plum makes a nice hedge or screening plant. Some dwarf varieties are popular as groundcovers.

➤ *C. grandiflora* 'Boxwood Beauty,' up to 2 feet. A compact, dense, evergreen shrub with deep green foliage and thorns. An excellent low hedge plant that requires full sun to partial shade. Zone 9.

➤ *C. grandiflora* 'Fancy,' Fancy Natal Plum, up to 6 feet. This is a spiny, evergreen shrub with fragrant white flowers followed by fruit. It tolerates seaside conditions and requires full sun to partial shade. Zone 9.

➤ *C. grandiflora* 'Green Carpet,' 13 inches. A dense, evergreen groundcover with fragrant white flowers followed by fruit. Requires full sun to partial shade. Zone 9.

➤ *C. grandiflora* 'Tuttlei,' Tuttle Natal Plum, up to 3 feet. This dense evergreen shrub has a spread of about 5 feet with fragrant white flowers followed by red fruit. It requires full sun to partial shade. Zone 9.

Carypteros × clandonensis
Blue Mist
2 to 4 feet
A deciduous shrub that has many stems of gray-green leaves and small blue flow-

ers on tips of growth. The flowers appear midsummer to first frost. In cold areas of the United States, blue mist usually freezes to the ground. It tolerates cold weather and drought conditions, but does not do well in the desert areas. Requires full sun. Zone 5.

Cassia artemisioides
Feathery Cassia
4 to 5 feet
An evergreen shrub with an open habit of growth. It has gray, needlelike leaflets that are 1 inch long with yellow, fragrant flowers. Requires full sun. Zone 8.

Cassia corymbosa
Flowery Senna
4 to 8 feet
A large shrub with 4 to 6 oval, bright green leaflets and profuse sprays of bowl-shaped, rich yellow flowers appearing in late summer. This Argentinian beauty grows best in protected areas. Zone 8.

Cassia Sturtii
Sturt's Cassia
5 feet
This evergreen shrub with gray-green foliage has yellow flowers. It tolerates drought conditions and requires full sun. Zone 8.

Ceanothus spp.
Wild Lilac
8 to 25 feet
This evergreen shrub has flowers that come in colors of blue, white or purple. The flowers are small, but they bloom

Flowery Senna.

William D. Adams

in mass for a strong effect. Because many of these are native to the western part of the United States, they tolerate dry and cold conditions well.

➢ *C.* × 'Concha,' Concha Wild Lilac, 8 feet. An evergreen shrub with a spread equal to its height. It has dark blue flowers. Once this plant is established, the concha has good drought tolerance. It requires full sun. Zone 8.

➤ *C.* × 'Frosty Blue,' Frosty Blue Wild Lilac, 9 feet. This evergreen shrub is drought resistant once it is established. Deep blue flowers with a frosty appearance. It requires full sun. Zone 8.

➤ *C. griseus horizontalis,* Carmel Creeper, 18 to 30 inches. This evergreen shrub is grown in the warmer areas of the United States with a spread of 8 feet. It has light blue, 1-inch flowers and grows best on dry banks. Requires full sun. Zone 8.

➤ *C.* × 'Julia Phelps,' Julia Phelps Wild Lilac, up to 7 feet. Once established, this evergreen shrub is quite drought tolerant. It has indigo-blue flower clusters. Requires full sun. Zone 8.

➤ *C.* × 'Ray Hartman', 20 feet. This large shrub can be trained to a small tree. It has blue flowers and good drought tolerance, once established. Zone 8.

Cestrum nocturnum
Night-Blooming Jasmine
5 to 10 feet
An evergreen shrub that has small white flowers that are night-blooming and very fragrant, almost an overpowering aroma. It has moderate drought tolerance once established and requires full sun to partial shade. Zone 9.

Chaenomeles japonica 'Minerva'
Minerva Flowering Quince
3 feet
This low-growing, deciduous shrub has red flowers in the early spring that appear before its leaves. These flowers can be used in flower arrangements. It requires full sun. Zone 5.

Cistus spp.
Rock Rose
Variable
A drought-tolerant, evergreen shrub that grows well in poor soils. It also tolerates heat and wind, and can be used as a seashore plant. It is sometimes used on banks, as a groundcover and as a transition plant. The flowers resemble old-fashioned open, single roses.

➤ *C.* × *hybridus (C. corbariensis),* White Rock Rose, 2 to 4 feet. An evergreen shrub with a spread equal to its height. It has fragrant white flowers and gray-green, crinkly leaves. It requires full sun. Zone 8.

➤ *C. ladanifer (C. maculatus),* Crimson Spot Rock Rose, 4 feet. The evergreen shrub has 3-inch white flowers with a red center. It grows as wide as it grows tall and requires full sun. Zone 8.

➤ *C.* × *purpureus,* Orchid Rock Rose, 4 feet. This makes a good plant for a seaside planting. It is an evergreen shrub with orchid-pink flowers with a red center. The underside of the leaves are gray. Requires full sun. Zone 8.

Coleonema album
White Breath-of-Heaven
5 feet
This shrub requires full sun and good drainage. It is an evergreen shrub with small white flowers that spreads as much as its height. Zone 9.

Coleonema pulchrum
(Diosma pulchrum)
Pink Breath-of-Heaven
5 to 6 feet
The flowers are small, pink stars on up-right branches. This shrub requires full sun to partial shade. Zone 9.

Convolvulus spp.
Morning Glory
Variable
A great groundcover, this plant is some-times used on dry banks or on a trellis where it shades walls—and saves energy. There are more than 1,000 species. It grows best in a well-draining soil—including Florida or Texas sand areas. In Florida, it grows best in full sun.

➤ *C. Cneorum,* Bush Morning Glory, 2 to 8 feet. A shrub-type growth habit, with a width as much as its height. It has wide, silver-gray leaves that are 1 to 2 inches long. The flowers are pink or white with yellow throats. It blooms most of the year, from May through September or October. Requires partial shade to full sun.

➤ *C. mauritanicus,* 1 to 3 feet. A ground type of morning glory that is an evergreen. Equal spread to its height. The round gray-green leaves are 1 to 1-½ inches long. It has attractive lavender-blue, 1- to 2-inch flowers from June to November. You should trim them back in early spring to keep them from getting woody. Zone 8.

Coprosma Kirkii
2 to 3 feet
A small, evergreen shrub that normally spreads an equal or greater amount than its height. It grows on horizontal stems from the base. The dense leaves are on small branches. It requires full sun to partial shade and will tolerate seaside conditions. Zone 8.

Cordia Boissieri
5 to 12 feet
This large shrub to small tree has gray-green leaves that are rough to the touch. The white flowers are 2 to 3 inches wide with a yellow throat. Blooms come in April through September. It makes a good desert plant. Water well to first establish, then when needed in the summer. Zone 8–10.

Cordyline indivisa
(Dracaena indivisa)
Blue Dracaena
20 feet
An evergreen plant with 6-foot sword-like leaves that have attractive white flower clusters. Good drought tolerance

once established and takes the coastal conditions well. Zone 9.

Correa × *'Dusley Bell's'*
Australian Fuchsia
3 feet
An evergreen shrub with continuous red blossoms. This plant is adaptable to many conditions and spreads out with growth equal to its height. It doesn't grow well in Florida.

Cotoneaster spp.
Cotoneaster
Some varieties are evergreen shrubs, while others are deciduous shrubs. Most have small leaves with large amounts of very small white or pink flowers that are followed by red fruits for winter color. Adaptable in most climates. Some of the lower groundcover types seem to lose the will to live (!) in the desert heat, however.

- ➤ *C. apiculatus,* Cranberry Cotoneaster, 4 feet. A low-growing, deciduous shrub that has pink flowers in the spring followed by red berries. It requires full sun. Zone 5.

- ➤ *C. congestus* 'Likiang,' 3 feet. This slow-growing evergreen has arching branches with small pink flowers followed by red berries. It requires full sun. Zone 5.

- ➤ *C. Dammeri* 'Coral Beauty.' An evergreen shrub with prostrate branches that spread several feet.

It has small, white flowers followed by berries. It requires full sun. Zone 6.

- ➤ *C. Dammeri* 'Lowfast,' 12 feet. A dense, evergreen groundcover spreading from 8 to 10 feet. It has white flowers followed by red berries. Requires full sun to partial shade. Zone 6.

- ➤ *C. divaricatus,* 6 feet. This upright, deciduous shrub has pink flowers followed by red berries for excellent fall colors. It can be used as a hedge or a screen plant and requires full sun. Zone 4.

- ➤ *C. glaucophyllus,* Bright Bead Cotoneaster, 6 feet. An evergreen shrub with an arching growth habit. It has white flower clusters followed by orange berries. It requires full sun. Zone 7.

- ➤ *C. horizontalis,* Rock Cotoneaster, 4 feet. A deciduous shrub with a fanlike spreading habit. It has pink flowers with red berries. A good plant for wall coverings. It requires full sun. Zone 5.

- ➤ *C. lacteus (C. Parneyi),* Red Clusterberry, 8 to 10 feet. This evergreen shrub has arching branches and white flowers followed by berries. It makes an excellent espalier or hedge plant. Requires full sun. Zone 7.

➤ *C. salicifolius* 'Repens,' Carpet Cotoneaster, 12 inches. An evergreen to semi-evergreen shrub spreading to 6 feet. It has willowlike foliage with white flowers and red berries. Requires full sun to partial shade. Zone 6.

Cytisus spp.
Broom Shrub
Variable

A fast-growing shrub of the pea family. The evergreen or deciduous shrub can tolerate very tough conditions such as wind, sun, and salt from the seashore. It does require good drainage and tolerates poor soil. The broom shrub can self sow and become a weed, if not watched closely. Grows best in lower California, Texas and Florida.

➤ *C. Canariensis,* Canary Island Broom, 6 to 8 feet. This evergreen shrub grows 5 to 6 feet wide and bears fragrant, yellow flowers and green leaves. It requires full sun. Zone 8.

➤ *C. × Dallimorei* 'Burkwoodii,' Burkwood's Broom, 6 to 8 feet. An evergreen shrub in warm climates with an upright habit. It bears sprays of carmine flowers in spring and early summer. Requires full sun. Zone 6.

➤ *C. racemosus (Genista racemosa),* Sweet Broom, up to 6 feet. A fast-growing, evergreen shrub with masses of bright, yellow flowers in the spring. It tolerates heat and drought well and requires full sun. Zone 8.

➤ *C. scoparius* 'Moonlight,' 6 to 8 feet. An evergreen shrub, this pale yellow scotch broom tolerates droughts well, once established. It requires full sun. Zone 6.

Dodonaea viscosa
Hopseed Bush
10 to 15 feet

This evergreen shrub, sometimes a small tree, has native varieties of Arizona and of the southwestern United States. It has a quick-growing, upright growth with 4-inch-long green leaves. The flowers are insignificant, but are followed by showy, pink-orange winged fruit. It tolerates the warm desert areas and requires full sun. Zone 8.

➤ *D. viscosa* 'Purpurea,' Purple Hopseed Bush, up to 15 feet. A fast-growing evergreen with the same spread as its height. It has bronze-green foliage that turns dark in the winter. It requires full sun to partial shade. Zone 8.

Elaeagnus multiflora
Cherry Elaeagnus
5 to 6 feet

A deciduous shrub whose leaves have a gray-green upperside and a brownish color underneath. Cherry Elaeagnus has yellow-green flowers followed by small fruit that resemble olives. It will tolerate cold, heat, and drought once established.

Elaeagnus pungens
Silverberry
5 to 15 feet
This evergreen shrub has an upright, angular growth pattern. It should be trimmed to keep in an attractive shape. The silverberry has silver-dotted, gray-green leaves with rust or brown scales on the twigs and leaves, and red, ½-inch fruit. It will tolerate extreme heat, wind, and drought once established. Requires full sun to partial shade. Zone 7.

Eriogonum **spp.**
Ornamental Buckwheat
Up to 4 feet
A shrublike perennial. It is *not* the food grain. It has small flowers in long clusters of many colors that age to a rust color. Some work well in flower arrangements. This plant needs good drainage and requires full sun. Native species in the West, Southwest, and Southeast. Zone 9.

Escallonia **spp.**
5 to 6 feet
This glossy, green-leaved, evergreen shrub has small flowers in pink, red, or white. It thrives in coastal areas and tolerates constant wind and sun, along with desert conditions. Once established, this plant has a moderate drought tolerance. It makes a good

Silverberry.

hedge, screen, or foundation plant. A South American group.

➤ *E.* × *exoniensis* 'Fradesi,' Pink Princess Escallonia, 4 to 6 feet. With color most of the year during the warm months, this evergreen shrub thrives in the coastal areas. It requires full sun. Zone 8.

➤ *E.* × 'Newport,' Newport Dwarf Escallonia, 30 inches. A slow-growing evergreen with rose red terminal flowers. It tolerates coastal conditions well and makes an excellent foundation shrub when planted in full sun. Zone 8.

Euphorbiaceae

A large family of plants, from one of the most popular plants available, the poinsettia, to spurge, a common weed.

➤ *Synadenium grantii,* African Milk Bush, 6 to 8 feet. With thick, sausagelike branches that have a milky sap, this evergreen shrub has leaves that are 4 feet long with clusters of red blossoms on the tips of the branches. It requires full sun to partial shade. Zone 10.

➤ *Codiaeum variegatum,* Croton. One of the most colorful foliage plants in the world. It is sometimes used in planters for bright areas outdoors. It tolerates many soil types and must be protected from the frost. There are many named varieties. Some of these do well in full sun while others prefer partial shade. It has a moderate drought tolerance after being established. Zone 9.

➤ *Euphorbia lactea,* Milkstripe. A cactus lookalike, milkstripe has 3 to 4 angled stems with brown spines. This plant has a milky sap in the stems when cut. It grows in a candelabrum shape and tolerates many soil types. Once established, you can water on rare occasions. It requires full sun. Zone 10.

➤ *E. milii,* Crown of Thorns. The stems and branches are densely armed with 1-inch spines on this plant. The leaves are on the new growth with bright red or pink bracts. It requires a well-drained soil and has excellent drought tolerance. Zone 9.

➤ *E. pulcherrima,* Poinsettia. The popular Christmas season plant, with a light, evergreen color. The bracts are modified leaves that color to red and pink. They do get injured in frost, but tolerate many types of well draining soil. Requires full sun. Native of tropical Central America. Zone 9.

Genista spp.
Broom
Variable

A deciduous shrub whose green branches give it an evergreen appearance. It has an abundance of sweetpea-type, bright yellow flowers in the spring and through early summer. Broom can be used on banks or as groundcover; or where rocky soils predominate. It does require full sun to partial shade in very hot areas. Zone 6.

Grevillea spp.
Variable

The *robusta* was discussed in the tree selection section of this book, but it should also be mentioned as a member of the shrub group.

➤ *G.* 'Noelli,' 5 feet. This shrub can be trimmed into a low hedge with a spread equal to its height. It has horizontal branching and 1-inch needle-like leaves with clusters of white and pink flowers in the spring. 'Noelii' requires full sun with a moderate drought tolerance. Zone 9.

Hardenbergia violacea
Variable

An evergreen, shrubby, vining plant seen in the warmer parts of the United States. It blooms in shades of bright purple and is sometimes grown over fences or arbors. This plant tolerates wind and full sun. Zone 9.

Helianthemum nummularium
Sunrose
8 to 10 inches

This small evergreen shrub, which spreads up to 3 feet, has ¾-inch leaves that are 1 inch long. It comes in many varieties, some with single or double flowers in colors of red, rose, white, orange, or orange-yellow. The sunrose is great grown on banks or for rock gardens. It also has a good drought tolerance once it is established. Requires full sun. Zone 7.

Hesperaloe parviflora
Red Yucca
5 feet

This plant is similar to the yucca, with long, thin leaves of gray-green color. Has gently arching stalks tipped with red flowers. It has great drought tolerance and requires full sun. Texas native. Zone 6.

Heteromeles arbutifolia
6 to 10 feet

An evergreen shrub with dark, glossy green, feathery foliage. It has small white flowers in the summer followed by bright red berries, which attract birds, in the fall and winter season. The *arbutifolia* has good drought tolerance and requires full sun to partial shade. California native. Zone 7.

Red Yucca.

William D. Adams

Hibiscus rosa-sinensis
Chinese Hibiscus
5 to 15 feet

One of the world's most spectacular flowering evergreen shrubs with flowers coming in almost every color in the rainbow. Many named varieties available. They stand little frost, so are best planted in warm areas. It has a fair drought tolerance once mature. Full sun. Zone 9.

Hypericum patulum 'Hidcote'
5 to 6 feet

An evergreen shrub that grows best in warm areas with a 5-foot spread. With its 3-inch, golden-yellow flowers, this shrub makes a good border plant. It requires full sun. Zone 5.

Ilex spp.
Holly
Variable

This is a very large group of plants commonly used as landscape shrubs. Most are hardy and drought tolerant once established. Many are North American natives.

➤ *I. cornuta* 'Burfordii,' Burford Holly, 3 to 4 feet. A compact, evergreen shrub that produces red berries and makes a nice hedge plant. It requires full sun to partial shade. Zone 6.

➤ *I. cornuta* 'Rotunda,' Dwarf Chinese Holly, 3 feet. A dense, evergreen shrub that has a compact growth habit. An excellent foundation plant or low hedge. It requires full sun to partial shade. Zone 7.

➤ *I.* × 'Nellie R. Stevens,' Nellie R. Stevens Holly. An evergreen shrub to small tree that produces bright red berries. It requires full sun to partial shade. Zone 6.

➤ *I. vomitoria* 'Pride of Houston,' Yaupon Holly, 20 feet. With its upright growth habit, this evergreen shrub to small tree has scarlet berries. It makes a good screen or hedge plant and requires full sun to partial shade. Zone 7.

➤ *I. vomitoria* 'Stokes Dwarf' or 'Stokes Yaupon,' 18 to 24 inches. An evergreen shrub that self fertilizes. It produces red berries and makes a great border or low foundation plant. Requires full sun to partial shade. Zone 7.

Juniperus spp.
Juniper
Variable

The juniper group is very large, with small flat-growing shrubs to large tree types. An evergreen with almost needle-like or scalelike foliage. Many have low watering needs. Because they are cold hardy and come in so many different forms, junipers fit in many landscapes. Plant in a well-drained soil and give reasonable care. Requires full sun with partial shade in the hottest areas of the United States. *J. horizontalis* is a native of the Northwest and northern central United States.

➤ *J. chinensis* 'Alba,' Variegated Prostrate Juniper, 18 inches. An evergreen shrub spreading 4 to 5 feet. In very hot areas it has a creamy white variegation and is sun sensitive. Requires full sun to partial shade. Zone 5.

➤ *J. chinensis* 'Bluepoint,' 3 feet. This evergreen shrub has a broad, pyramidal shape without shearing. Upright growth habit. Requires full sun. Zone 4.

➤ *J. chinensis* 'Robusta Queen,' 15 feet. A slow-growing evergreen with a good natural shape. There is little need to keep it sheared. It does require full sun. Zone 5.

➤ *J. chinensis* 'San Jose' *(J. japonica)*, 18 to 24 inches. This evergreen shrub can spread 5 to 6 feet with new blue-green growth that becomes darker green when more mature. This plant makes an excellent bonsai. Requires full sun. Zone 4.

➤ *J. chinensis* 'Glauca,' Blue Sargent Juniper, 15 inches. With dense blue foliage and an 8 to 10 foot spread, this evergreen shrub makes an excellent groundcover. Full sun to partial shade. Zone 4.

➤ *J. chinensis* 'Seaspray,' 15 inches. An evergreen shrub that can spread up to 6 feet with blue-green foliage. It is great for those hot areas in your

Shore Juniper.

landscape and makes a good groundcover. Requires full sun. Zone 5.

➤ *J. chinensis* 'Spearmint,' 15 feet. A dense, evergreen shrub that has a columnar growth habit with bright green foliage. It requires little maintenance. Full sun. Zone 5.

➤ *J. conferta* 'Blue Pacific,' Shore Juniper, 12 inches. Grown in the cold areas of the United States, with a 4- to 8-foot spread, this evergreen shrub makes an excellent seaside groundcover. It has blue-green foliage and requires full sun to partial shade. Zone 6.

➤ *J. horizontalis* 'Bar Harbor,' up to 8 inches. An evergreen shrub that has a mounding growth habit. The dense, slate-blue foliage will turn a plum color in colder weather. Most popular in the cold areas of the United States. Requires full sun. Zone 4.

➤ *J. horizontalis* 'Prince of Wales,' up to 6 inches. This evergreen shrub has a 10-foot spread with apple green foliage that turns purple in colder weather. It is very cold hardy and requires full sun. Zone 3.

➤ *J. horizontalis* 'Wiltonii,' Blue Rug Juniper, 4 to 5 feet. An evergreen shrub with a 6-foot spread and frosty blue foliage. It makes an excellent groundcover. Requires full sun to partial shade. Zone 4.

➤ *Juniperus × media* 'Hetzi' (*Juniperus chinensis* 'Hetzi'), up to 15 feet. This evergreen shrub has a fountainlike appearance with blue-gray foliage. Perfect for mass plantings. It requires full sun. Zone 4.

➤ *J. × media Pfitzeriana,* Green Pfitzer Juniper, up to 5 feet. This evergreen shrub has arching branches in a ten-foot spread. Gray-green leaves. It requires full sun. Zone 4.

➤ *J. × media Pfitzeriana glauca (Juniperus chinensis),* Blue Pfitzer, 8 feet. A fast-growing evergreen with a 10-foot spread and blue foliage on arching branches. It makes an

excellent contrast plant in the landscape. Plant in full sun. Zone 4.

Lagerstroemia indica
Crape Myrtle
Up to 20 feet

A deciduous shrub with some varieties that can be trained into trees. The flowers appear similar to the lilac: small, 1-inch clusters of 8 to 12 inches that bloom over a long period, from May, June, July, and sometimes again in September. Many varieties of colors in the red, pink, lavender, and white ranges. It has a smooth, pale brown or gray bark that often peels and shows pinkish brown on the new bark. Crape myrtle should be pruned in the dormant (winter) season. The small, light green leaves later provide some fall color. It does require full sun. Zone 7.

Crape Myrtle.

Lavandula **spp.**
Lavender
2 to 4 feet
A perennial shrub/herb with gray-green leaves and fragrant flowers. Yes, this is the plant used in sachets and perfumes. It can be used as a border plant or as a low hedge and should be pruned after blooming to keep the plant in bounds. Lavender needs little water or fertilizer and should be planted in full sun to partial shade.

➤ *L. angustifolia,* English Lavender. With two-inch, narrow, gray leaves

A striking contrast, Cenizo (Texas Sage) and Yucca (Adam's Needle).

William D. Adams

and delicate purple flowers on spikes. Blooms in spring through summer.

➤ *L. dentata,* French Lavender. French lavender has toothed, gray-green leaves with lavender/purple flower clusters. There is a gray-white down on the young foliage.

➤ *L. stoechas,* Spanish Lavender. Gray-green, narrow leaves and clusters of dark purple flowers topped by a tuft of purple bracts.

Leucophyllum frutescens
Texas Sage, Texas Ranger, Cenizo
4 to 8 feet, sometimes taller
An evergreen shrub of gray-white foliage and bill-shaped, rose flowers. A striking plant, great for desert, heat, dry, wind, and high pH soil. It requires full sun. Texas and Southwest native. Zone 8.

Mahonia **spp.**
Mahonia
6 to 12 feet
An evergreen shrub that is sometimes classified as barberry *(Berberis)*. Its stems do not have spines, but the leaves do have sharp-toothed edges. The flowers are yellow in spikelike clusters. It takes heat, sun or shade, and drought.

➤ *M. aquifolium,* Oregon Grape, 6 to 8 feet. This evergreen shrub spreads slowly by underground stems with leaves 4 to 10 inches long. Glossy, spiny toothed leaflets are deep green. The new leaves are a bronze color, the same color in the fall, before falling. Native to Pacific Northwest. Zone 5.

➤ *M. pinnata,* California Holly Grape. This plant is spinier than the Oregon Grape with crinkled leaves. California native.

➤ *M. repens,* Creeping Mahonia. This plant has underground stems that grow up to 3 feet. Native to Northwest and California. Zone 5.

Myoporum parvifolium
3 inches

This prostrate shrub can spread up to 6 feet with narrow leaves that are ½ to 1 inch long. The small, white and pink flowers bloom in the summer, and are followed by purple berries. It requires full sun. Zone 9.

Nandina domestica
Heavenly Bamboo
4 to 8 feet

This evergreen shrub has an upright growth pattern and lacy, compound leaves. Along with its deciduous foliage that creates a lovely red fall color are small, white flowers in long terminal panicles, followed by bright red berries ¼ inch in diameter. It requires full sun to partial shade. Zone 8.

Nerium Oleander
Oleander
8 to 25 feet

This tall, almost broad, evergreen shrub has lance-shaped leaves. The flowers

Heavenly Bamboo (Nandina).

come in colors of red, pink, or white. A perfect seaside plant and it makes an excellent screen at the edge of properties. The biggest problem this plant has to

Oleander.

contend with is the oleander caterpillar. There are dwarf varieties that are 3 to 5 feet tall. The flowers and leaves are poisonous to eat. It requires full sun. Zone 9.

Osmanthus spp.
5 to 20 feet

An evergreen shrub with leathery, sometimes glossy, leaves. Once this plant is established, it has good drought tolerance and grows well in well-draining soils.

> ➤ *O. fragrans,* Sweet Olive, 8 to 10 feet. A compact habit of growth with leaves that are medium green in color and up to 4 inches long. It also has small, white flowers that bloom most of the year. Requires full sun. Zone 8.

> ➤ *O. heterophyllus,* Holly Leaf Osmanthus, 6 to 8 feet. Its hollylike appearance makes this plant an excellent hedge plant. It has dark green leaves and an upright growth habit. It requires full sun. Zone 7.

Pavonia spp.
Pavonia, Rock Rose
3 to 4 feet

Small shrub with blooms that resemble wild rose blooms, in pink shades. Tolerates many kinds of soils, but needs good drainage. Sun to partial shade. Southwest native.

Pittosporum tobira
Pittosporum
5 to 20 feet

This evergreen shrub spreads 5 to 8 feet. The creamy white to yellow flowers have a pleasant fragrance. It makes a good hedge or screening plant, though it is also used in mass plantings. Once established, this plant has good drought tolerance. Zone 8.

Plumbago spp.
Plumbago
2 to 6 feet

An evergreen to semi-evergreen shrub with a sprawling 4- to 10-foot wide growth. Pale blue or white flowers. It needs good drainage. Makes an excellent background or screen plant. Sun to partial shade. Zone 9.

Protea spp.
Protea
Variable

An evergreen shrub to tree from South Africa with showy flower heads and colorful bracts. Excellent for cut flowers. The protea should be watered until well established, then it's unneeded. Requires full sun. Zone 9.

Pyracantha spp.
Firethorn, Pyracantha
Up to 20 feet

Often used as an espalier, this evergreen shrub or climber is very thorny. It has white flowers with masses of red-orange, berrylike fruit. Zone 4.

Rhaphiolepis indica
India Hawthorn
5 feet
A shrub with a compact growth habit
and pink or white flowers. Makes an excellent landscape plant. It tolerates most
soils and has a good drought tolerance.
Zone 7.

Rosa spp.
Rose
Variable
Most growers realize that the rose group
is a high-maintenance plant, but some
roses are rather tough. Some wild rose

India Hawthorn.

ROSES IN THE WATER-THRIFTY GARDEN

Roses are some of the most versatile plants in the landscape. While they require
more care than perhaps other garden plants, the rewards of beauty and fragrance
are worth it.

   Roses do require more water than some of the other selections for a water-
thrifty garden, and should be planted in your oasis area or near a water source. I
strongly recommend a drip irrigation system (see "Choosing a Water System") in
a rose garden for both good bloom and for water savings. Many of the climbers
and the antique rose varieties can survive, once established, on the natural rainfall
where there is moderate precipitation. Antique roses—roughly, those rose varieties existing or introduced up to the early 1900s—have often proven hardy to
drought, disease, and neglect. And they are increasingly coming back into circulation. Your local rose society is an excellent source of information and may have
some of the older varieties to share.

   Important too is good drainage. You may find it helpful to build a raised bed
to accommodate your roses, especially if water tends to stand in the planting bed.
Landscape timber—3 or 4 timbers per side—can be purchased at most building
supply stores.

   Roses grow best in a slightly acid soil (5.8 to 6.8 pH). If the soil is too acid,
add 5 to 6 pounds of dolomite limestone per hundred quare feet of rose bed; and
if the soil is too alkaline, add 1 pound of sulphur per hundred square feet.

Scott Ogden

Antique roses make great garden investments, both for their practical hardiness and their beauty. Here, 'Mrs. B. R. Cant.'

varieties, antique roses, shrub roses, climbers, and others have moderate watering needs. Requires full sun. Zone 4.

SOME ROSE SELECTIONS

Rose	Notes	Color	Height
Don Juan	climber	deep red	10 ft.
Cherokee (R. laevigata)	naturalized/ climber	white	15 ft.
Lady Banks' Rose (R. banksia)	antique climber	white, yellow	20 ft.
Swamp Rose (R. palustris)	native	deep pink	6 ft.

Rosmarinus officinalis
Rosemary
Up to 6 feet
A shrub/perennial and groundcover with narrow, aromatic leaves—dark green above and white to gray underneath. The flowers are lavender-blue, ½ inch long, blooming in the winter and spring. Upright and prostrate varieties available. Yes, this is the herb used in seasoning. Rosemary requires good drainage and tolerates poor soil and drought. Zone 7.

Scaevola × 'Mauve Clusters'
Fan Flowers
In warm climates, up to 3 to 5 feet

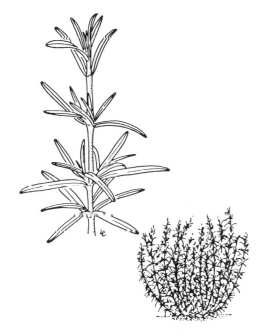

Rosemary.

This plant was introduced by the University of California, Santa Cruz. A spread as wide as its height. The fan flowers have blue flowers when in bloom. It tolerates a mild frost and drought conditions. Requires full sun. Zone 8.

Taxus spp.
Yew
10 to 50 feet
An evergreen, slow-growing shrub with dark green, flat leaves. It is often used in hedges. Tolerates an average soil. The yew requires full sun to partial shade. Some native North American species. Zone 4.

Yucca spp.
Yucca
Variable
Native plants—from South to Southwest—characterized by swordlike, rigid, dark green leaves, spined. Often have fragrant flower stalks.

➢ *Y. filimentosa,* Adam's Needle, to 10 feet. Native to Southeast. Two- to 3-foot-long dark green leaves, clumping, with wonderful and fragrant white blossoms perched above on its stalks. Zone 5.

ANNUALS, PERENNIALS, AND VINES

ANNUALS

Even though annuals may not seem to fit into the water-thrifty garden, they absolutely do and must because of the beauty and color they offer. Remember, we don't have to have just rocks and cacti in a water-efficient garden. In the spring, beautiful pansies, with their brilliantly painted faces, add vibrance to the flower bed, while in the warm summer months, zinnias and marigolds bring bright, sunny splashes.

It is this change of mood in the landscape—different textures, colors, and shapes—that is the special contribution of annuals. Even small backyards or balconies can have this color difference. Just as artists use colors for their paintings, we can use annuals to create warmth—in red, orange, or yellow—or for a cool effect, colors such as white, gray, blue, or violet. Or, simply use annuals as accents.

Annuals may not come to mind as a first choice for a water-thrifty garden, but they should not be excluded. They do add so much to the garden. Out of the many possible annuals, I include here twelve trusty and hardy annuals that can handle drought to get you started.

TWELVE TOP ANNUALS

Amaranthus spp.
Amaranthus
Vivid foliage color—mostly red and yellow-green—in sword-shaped leaves. To

A colorful and informal perennial border of coreopsis and salvia, with yarrow in the background.

William D. Adams

3 feet tall. Plant after frost has passed. Germinates in 10 to 20 days; tolerates heat and drought. 'Jospeh's Coat' is a popular variety.

Celosia spp.
Cockscomb
Plant after all danger of frost has passed. Brilliant colors—deep red, pink, or gold—in soft plumes or as velvety "cockscombs." Around 2 feet tall. Germinates in 15 days.

Gazania spp.
Gazania
Germinates in 21 days. Requires full sun. Tolerates dry sandy soils. Bright colors of pink, red, yellow, and orange

in a large bloom. Some varieties have wildly striped petals. About 1½ feet tall.

Gomphrena globusa
Globe Amaranth, Gomphrena
Germinates in 15 to 20 days; grows in well-drained soil; tolerates heat and drought. The most familiar color is an intense fuchsia, but globe amaranth has shades of orange, ivory, and raspberry red, all very effective in mass plantings. Grows in clumps, about 2 feet tall.

Helianthus annuus
Sunflower
Cheery, easy-to-grow annuals that everyone knows—a large flower head with a ring of lemon-yellow petals. Grows very tall, to 8 or 10 feet, so best to keep at

James Donovan

Annuals can bring brightness to the garden. Here, many-hued zinnias complement the perennial black-eyed susans in the background.

the back of a garden planting. Takes full sun. Seeds popular with the birds, too.

Helichrysum bracteatum
Strawflower
Germinates in 7 to 10 days. Plant after frost has passed. Good range of bright, warm colors. Good cut flower. Grows to 2½ feet.

Pelargonium spp.
Geranium
Popular container plant. Pink, white, fuchsia, and scarlet clusters of flowers on stem. Bright lime green leaves are attractive foliage. Many differently scented varieties. Grows to 2 feet.

Portulaca grandiflora
Moss Rose
Low to the ground or hugging, 6 to 8 inches tall. Germinates in 10 to 15 days. Sow seeds after last frost. Will tolerate and grow well in heat and drought. Again, a variety of vivid colors,

from yellow to peach to magenta. Some varieties have multiple-petaled flowers.

Senecio cineraria
Dusty Miller
Germinates in 10 to 14 days. Prefers dry, sandy soil. Plant in full sun to partial shade. Silver/gray velvety and lacelike foliage. Makes a good buffer (or transition plant) between bright flowering plants.

Moss Rose.

James Donovan

Tagetes spp.
Marigolds

Another trusty annual that takes the summer heat of Southwest, Texas, and the Southeast. It's a Mexican native. Good in massed plantings. Bright yellow and orange in pom-pom heads. Finely cut, dark green foliage for good contrast. Grows 2 to 3 feet tall.

Vinca major
Vinca, Periwinkle

Five-petaled, pink-violet (and white) flowers with glossy dark green leaves. Germinates in 15 to 20 days; flowers best in full sun. Will reseed for plants the next year.

Zinnia elegans
Zinnia

An annual favorite. Germinates in 5 to 10 days. Give them room so they can have good air circulation. This will help to prevent powdery mildew. Grows 2 to 3 feet tall. Good heat and drought tolerance. Bright colors of pink, yellow,

Vinca.

A WILDFLOWER MEADOW

The idea of having your own wildflower meadow has become very popular recently and makes sense from a water conservation viewpoint. Since wildflowers are by definition surviving on their own with only natural rainfall, a meadow in your backyard can be a beautiful way to cut back on water use. Because of the increased popularity, most gardening catalogs and garden supply centers offer wildflower seed mixes for any part of the country—East, Northwest, Plains, etc. However, there's also the popular but mistaken notion that you can simply toss your seed out to the wind and have a colorful garden in the spring. You still need to make soil preparation, because unless the seed makes contact with the soil— along with moisture to establish and sunlight—it's just a waste of time. Clear the desired area of competing plants, cultivate it, and contribute nutrients (organic material) to the soil just as you would when making a first garden or establishing transplants. Your local nurseryman or extension agent can make suggestions on wildflowers that will work for your region.

orange, etc. in single-petaled as well as the more common multiple-petaled varieties.

PERENNIALS

The great advantage of perennials is the fact that they are a lasting garden investment, by definition living more than two years. The right selections will give the gardener beauty for a long time with relatively little effort.

Many gardeners bypass perennials because they are not always as showy as annuals upon first planting. Since perennials do live longer than annuals, they will require more fertilizer and care over the years. Yet in the long run, the work requirements are less because there is less replacement time, less expense, and less effort. The rewards for growing perennials are abundant, with lots of color for the water-thrifty garden.

TOP PERENNIALS AND VINES

Acanthus mollis
2 to 4 feet
This evergreen or deciduous perennial has large leaves, up to 2 feet long, that are deeply cut arising from rhizomes. The spike of white flowers are tinged with rose or purple. It grows best in shade but can tolerate some sun in mild summer areas of the U.S. Like many flowering plants, it should be mulched.

Achillea spp.
Yarrow
Variable
This perennial has fernlike leaves and flowers in daisylike clusters. It is sometimes used as a groundcover. The taller varieties are used as background plants in the landscape. The yarrow will tolerate drought once it is established and requires full sun. Zone 3.

➤ *A. filipendulina,* Fern-leaf Yarrow, 4 to 6 feet. This plant has dark green leaves with yellow flowers that are excellent for cutting.

➤ *A. millefolium,* Common Yarrow, up to 3 feet. There are a number of named varieties of the common yarrow. It is sometimes considered a weed. *A. millefolium* is not an American native, but it has

Yarrow.

Walter K. Taylor

naturalized in much of the country. The yarrows come in colors of red, yellow, pink, salmon, and shades of all of these.

Agapanthus spp.
Lily of the Nile

This perennial has evergreen, straplike leaves and clumps of mostly blue flowers. Some of the white-flowered agapanthus are more drought-tolerant than they appear.

➤ *A. africanus,* Lily of the Nile. This has large clusters of blue flowers on 24-inch stems. It requires full sun to partial shade. Zone 8.

➤ *A. africanus albus,* White, Lily of the Nile.

➤ *A. africanus* 'Peter Pan,' 12- to 15-inch stems. Blue. Full sun to partial shade. Zone 8.

Agave victoriae-reginae
Queen Victoria Maguey
1 to 2 feet

Small agave, a Mexican native. Many thick leaves circling out from center, almost like an artichoke. Very few spines—a plus among the agaves. Texas and Southwest. Zone 9. (See also shrub chapter.)

Aloe spp.
Aloe
1 to 3 feet

A succulent perennial that fits well in a rock garden setting. Once this plant is established, watering becomes necessary only in severe drought conditions. The aloe does require full sun to partial shade. Often used in the kitchen for its chemical healing properties for burns. Zone 9.

Alyssum saxatile
(Aurinia saxatilis)
Alyssum
10 to 15 inches

Full sun for best blooms, plant in the early spring. Most nurseries have transplants. The alyssum is great in rock

This Texas garden uses "desert" elements in a soft way, uniting the artichoke-like agave Queen Victoria Maguey with sedum as groundcover with the bright red Salvia greggii *as an accent.*

William D. Adams

gardens and in perennial flower beds. They are easy to grow and have bright yellow, purple, and white flowers.

Antennaria rosea
Cat's Foot or Pussytoes
1 foot
This makes an excellent rock garden plant or groundcover. It has gray-green, 1-inch leaves with a flower stalk that is about a foot tall with rose-colored flower clusters. A native of the Northwest, down to California. It requires full sun. Zone 7.

Antigonon leptopus
Coral Vine
Variable
This deciduous vine from Mexico is fast growing with pink, white, or red sprays of flowers. An excellent clinging vine for warm areas of the United States. It can be invasive and will need pruning to keep it in bounds. Once established, watering can be forgotten. Zone 8.

Aptenia cordifolia
This perennial is used as a groundcover, often trailing or shrublike. The leaves are bright green and in the spring and early summer it has red flowers. Zone 6.

Aquilegia spp.
Columbine
1 to 2 feet
There are many native varieties of this woodland plant. The blooms are characterized by long spurs, and come in yellow, red, violet, blue, and white.

Good for rock gardens or naturalistic woods settings. Partial shade to shade. Needs good drainage.

➤ *A. canadensis,* Wild Columbine, 2 feet. Native plant of the East and Northeast, through upper South. The spring blooms have soft red spurs and yellow centers. Best in sandy, well-draining soil. Zone 5.

Asparagus densiflorus

➤ *Cv. Sprengeri* Even though this plant is in the lily family, it looks like a fern with its prickly, feathery foliage. It is a perennial with tuberous roots and small, white flowers followed by red berries. The sprengeri is often used in hanging baskets and as indoor plants. Its tuberlike root system keeps it alive during the dry periods. Requires full sun to partial shade. Zone 9.

➤ *Cv. Myersii* This plant has an erect green foxtail look to the stem and is more upright than the sprengeri.

Aspidistra elatior
Aspidistra
18 to 30 inches
This is also known as the Cast Iron Plant. Grows well in shade and has strap-shaped leaves. Many nurseries will carry small plants of the aspidistra. In the colder areas of the United States, mulch or keep in containers to protect from the winter cold. Zone 7.

Aster spp.
Aster

2 to 4 feet

This plant has summer and fall color of white, pink, blue, and purple in daisy-like blooms (it is a member of the *Compositae* family). Grows in rounded clumps, and when flowering is covered with blooms. Most nurseries have transplants. Plant about 3 feet in full sun in perennial beds. Really a carefree garden perennial. Many native species. Zone 5.

Baptisia australis
False Indigo

3 to 6 feet

A perennial with blue-green leaves that are 2- to 3-inch leaflets with clusters of deep blue flowers. Sometimes used in flower arrangements. It will tolerate

False Indigo.

many soil types. Native to Pennsylvania and the East down to the uppper Southeast. Zone 7.

Bergenia cordifolia
(*Saxifraga rubicunda*)

Up to 18 inches

A perennial evergreen that forms clumps of 24-inch widths and pink flower spikes. This plant makes a good edging plant, also an excellent groundcover for shade. Zone 4.

Bougainvillea spp.
(See chapter on shrubs.)

Caladium spp.
1 to 2 feet

The caladium grows best in shade to partial sun. Its long bulbs produce long leaves. In below-freezing areas of the United States, dig bulbs in fall after the leaves have died back. Store the bulbs in

Prairie Aster.

a dry area (above 60°F) until the ground warms in the spring. Colorful foliage makes this a landscape favorite.

Campsis radicans
(Bignonia radicans)
Trumpet Creeper
Variable

A deciduous, sometimes shrubby vine that climbs over trellis and walls and can reach 40 feet. Its 2- to 9-foot leaves are divided with trumpet-shaped, deep orange flowers. This vigorous grower can sometimes grow out-of-bounds and should be trimmed. One variety, Flava, has yellow, trumpet-shaped flowers. This vine requires full sun to partial shade. Native to East, Southeast, and Texas. Zone 5.

Canna × generalis
Canna
2 to 5 feet

Plant in full sun to partial shade. Blooms in spring through fall. The canna has colors of red, yellow, orange, pink, and white. It makes an excellent background plant. Set root divisions 18 inches apart in the spring. You will no doubt have to treat for leaf rollers. Prune old flowers out to increase blooms over a longer season.

Cerastium tomentosum
Snow-in-the-Summer
6 to 10 inches

This perennial has mats of white, silvery leaves 1-inch long with a 3-foot spread. The white flowers are ½ inch on a 6-inch stalk. It flowers in early summer and is often used as groundcover and in rock gardens. It requires full sun to partial shade and adjusts to the hot areas of Florida, Texas, Arizona, and southern California. Zone 3.

Ceratostigma plumbaginoides
(Ceratostigma Larpentiae)
Dwarf plumbago
12 Inches

A small perennial with bronze-green foliage that turns red in the fall. It has deep blue flowers and makes an excellent border plant. Requires full sun to

Canna.

Walter K. Taylor

partial shade and has good drought tolerance once established. Zone 5.

Chrysanthemum morifolium
Chrysanthemum
18 to 24 inches
Plant in full sun. Blooming (many are white, some are large with yellow centers) in early spring to fall color. Great as low border or in mass plantings. Need to be fertilized every 6 to 8 weeks with a bloomer-type fertilizer.

Clematis paniculata
Sweet Autumn Clematis
Variable
An easy-to-grow vine (as opposed to the preparation many *Clematis* require) with wonderfully fragrant small white blooms that cover the plant in summer. While not native to the Americas, it has naturalized in the South. Tolerates most soils and needs sun to partial shade. Zone 5.

Clytostoma callistegioides
(Bignonia violacea)
Lavender Trumpet Vine
5 feet
A vigorous evergreen vine from South America that climbs by tendrils, with trumpet-shaped, lavender flowers. Requires full sun to partial shade. This plant is often used on a trellis. Zone 9.

Convolvulus spp.
(See chapter on shrubs.)

Coreopsis spp.
Coreopsis, Golden Wave
Variable
A plant that looks somewhat like its relative, the sunflower. It has a yellow, daisylike flower and is very popular due to its reputation of carefree growth. These plants have been used on medium strips along highways. This gives one an idea of how tough these plants are. The coreopsis has good drought tolerance once established. They require full sun to partial shade. Zone 7.

➢ *C. grandiflora*, 2 to 3 feet. A native of the Plains, this plant has bright yellow flowers that are 2 to 3 inches wide. It flowers from May to November or until the first frost. It is often used as a cut flower. The grandiflora often grows as wide as its height. Zone 5.

➢ *C. verticillata*, 2 to 3 feet. A tall, perennial native with 2-inch yellow daisies that appear in summer through the fall. In the early sunrise, it has double, golden-yellow flowers. Excellent as cut flowers or can be used as a border plant. Requires full sun. 'Moonbeam' is an acclaimed cultivar. Zone 5.

Crinum bulbispermum
Crinum Lily
2 to 5 feet
Plant in full sun to partial shade. The crinum lily shows white flowers in the summer; some varieties have pink-white

flowers, with strap-shaped leaves. Also, plant in the fall or early spring. Zone 5.

Delosperma spp.
Ice Plant
12 inches
This mediterranean native has succulent leaves and daisylike flowers and a creeping growth habit.

> ➤ *D. Cooperi*. A low-growing succulent with textured green foliage. It has lavender blossoms most of the year. Makes an excellent groundcover for sunny locations. Zone 4.

> ➤ *D. nubigenum,* Yellow Ice Plant. A compact succulent with medium-green foliage and bright, yellow flowers. A great groundcover for sunny areas. Zone 5.

Ice Plant (D. Cooperi).

Dietes morea
African Iris
3 to 4 feet
An evergreen clumping perennial with long, stiff leaves that are flat and fan-shaped. It has branching flower stalks that produce an abundance of white, waxy flowers with orange, yellow, or brown markings. Some varieties have purple stippling. Cut off the old flower stalks and brown seed pods. The old flowers can be cut but as long as the stalks are green, they may keep producing more flowers. They tolerate wet and dry areas equally as well.

> ➤ *D. bicolor (Moraea bicolor),* Peacock Flower. An evergreen perennial with stiff, upright leaves, up to 30 inches. It has cream-colored flowers with maroon spots. It requires full sun. Zone 8.

> ➤ *D. vegeta (Moraea vegeta),* Butterfly Iris, 4 feet. This evergreen perennial with stiff, upright, fanning foliage has small irislike flowers. It requires full sun to partial shade. Zone 8.

Distictis buccinatoria
Scarlet Trumpet Vine
Variable
Massed with prolific clusters of 3- to 4-inch trumpet-shaped flowers of orange-yellow or red, turning to purple. An evergreen vine from Mexico that climbs by tendrils. Requires full sun to partial shade. Zone 9.

Echinacea purpurea
(Rudbeckia purpurea)
Purple Coneflower
3 to 4 feet

A perennial of the *Compositae* family that grows in clumps and blooms in summer and early fall. Native in the Midwest and East, down to the South. The purple flowers are large—up to 5 to 6 inches across—with distinctive "cone" centers. There is also a white variety. It tolerates most soil types and requires full sun. Zone 3.

Echinops exaltatus
Globe Thistle
3 to 4 feet

This perennial has a stiff, upright habit of growth with deeply cut, gray-green, prickly thistle leaves. The small blue flower clusters make nice cut flowers. It grows best with moderate amounts of moisture but can tolerate drought quite well once established. It also grows well in most soil types and should be planted in full sun. Zone 3.

Echium fastuosum
Pride of Madeira
6 feet

A multistemmed perennial of gray-green leaves and blue to purple flower spikes on the end of its branches. It tolerates drought well once established, although in dry areas, you may want to water some to keep it growing at its best. Zone 9.

Erigeron Karvinskianus
Santa Barbara Daisy, Mexican Daisy
10 to 20 inches

An evergreen perennial that spreads 20 to 30 inches wide with small, ¾-inch-

Purple Coneflower.

James Donovan

across blooms of white-pink, almost red. You may get all color at the same time. It blooms most of the year and tends to self-sow. This makes it somewhat weedy. This daisy grows in many different soil types and is used in hanging baskets, slopes, and even for wall coverings. It has excellent drought tolerance and requires full sun to partial shade. Zone 8.

Eschscholzia californica
California Poppy
1 to 2 feet
A western native, especially California, California poppy is useful when you want a more natural look in a wildflower garden. Bright orange flowers. Needs sun. More often annual; best to use that way.

Gaillardia grandiflora
Blanketflower
2 feet
Hardy and bright perennial, with distinctive composite-like flowers that have red-orange centers and bright yellow tips. Good for more informal, casual look. Naturalized in the Southwest and West. Zone 3.

Gelsimium sempervirens
Carolina Jasmine
10 to 20 feet
An evergreen that is a vine, moderate to fast grower. It has fragrant, yellow flowers. This makes an excellent trellis plant or can be grown on banks, arbors, and fences. Requires full sun with periodic waterings. Native to Southeast, Florida, over through Texas. Zone 6.

Hamelia patens
Firebush
4 feet
This large perennial to shrub lives up to its name with large sprays of vivid trumpet-shaped red blooms and sturdy, long red leaves. A Florida and Central/South America native that will also do well in Southern California and South Texas, as well as coastal portions of the South. Needs good drainage and sun to part sun. Zone 9.

Hedera canariensis
Algerian Ivy
This ivy makes a great groundcover and will also climb a trellis or up the side of a house. It has dark green leaves—and a larger leaf than most ivies have. Full sun to partial shade. Zone 9.

➢ Hedera canariensis 'Variegata,' Variegated Algerian Ivy. A vigorous, evergreen vine that is green with a cream-colored variegation. This showy groundcover is sometimes staked on a trellis or trimmed as a topiary. It requires full sun to partial shade. Zone 9.

Hedera helix
English Ivy
Another vigorous evergreen vine—associated fondly with the ivy-league schools. This versatile and handsome

English Ivy.

vine can cling to almost anything. It requires partial sun to full shade. Zone 5.

Helianthus Maximiliani
Maximilian Sunflower
10 feet

Because of its height, it's probably best to use this plant at the back of a garden design. Abundant, 3-inch-wide yellow flowers on tall stalks, blooming in late summer. Native to Plains through the East.

Helianthus salicifolius
3 to 10 feet

A perennial native of Texas, Oklahoma, Colorado, and Missouri, this clump-growing shrub has drooping leaves, 6 to 12 inches long, with bright yellow flowers that have bright centers. A good drought-tolerant plant once established. It requires full sun. Zone 8.

Helleborus spp.
Hellebore
1 to 3 feet

An evergreen, perennial shrub great for shade to partial shade. It has divided leaves with attractive flowers. Plant in an improved soil with good drainage. There are a number of good varieties to choose from. Although it has excellent drought tolerance, the hellebore should be watered during long, hot summers.

➤ *H. foetidus,* up to 18 inches. This shrub has divided leaves that are narrow and dark green. The green flowers with purple margins start to bloom in February through April. Sometimes they will self-seed after being established. Zone 7.

➤ *H. lividus corsicus,* Corsican Hellebore, up to 2 or 3 feet. Large clusters of long-lasting chartreuse flowers from late winter through spring in the southeastern United States and in the early spring in the northwestern United States. It also has divided leaves and requires full sun. Zone 8.

Hemerocallis spp.
Day Lily
1 to 4 feet

Plant in full sun to partial shade. Blooms (both single and double) in late spring to summer with flowers of yellow, orange, red, purple, pink, and off-white. Space the plants 24 inches apart; divide the clumps when they become crowded. Zone 4.

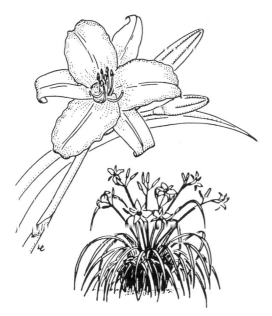

Daylily.

Hippeastrum × *johnsonii*
Amaryllis
12 to 24 inches
Striking flowers come in colors of red, pink, white and many striped varieties. Plant with half of the bulb above the ground, spaced 12 to 18 inches apart. Plant in full sun. Zone 7.

Iris spp.
Iris
1 to 4 feet
A large group of plants, many with creeping rhizomes, although some have bulbs. Many varieties also have the fanning, sword-shaped leaves.

➢ Bearded Iris, 2 to 4 feet. This is the most common iris grown, with hundreds of varieties in almost every imaginable color. It has gray-green,

sword-shaped leaves. Requires full sun to partial shade (in hot areas). Zone 3.

Lantana spp.
Lantana
2 to 5 feet
Plant in full sun. Flowers come in colors of lavender, yellow, pink, orange, and red. Most nurseries have small plants for sale. Plant after frost. A heavy mulching

The Bearded Iris has long been a favorite in cottage gardens and pairs well with roses, here in a Texas garden. 'Marie Pavie' is the white-blush rose next to it.

Scott Ogden

Lantana 'Confetti.'

can help give some protection in the southern part of the United States. Lantana is great for drought and heat tolerance. *L. montevidensis* is a wonderfully mounding perennial/shrub of soft lavender. Not a North American native,

Variegated Japanese Silver Grass.

but naturalized in South and parts of Southwest.

Liatris spicata
Gayfeather
2 to 3 feet
A grasslike perennial with a clump of narrow leaves and rose-purple flower stalks. Tolerates poor soil. Requires full sun. Native in the Northeast down through Southeast and South. Zone 3.

Lonicera spp.
Honeysuckle
Variable
Some varieties of these are evergreen, while others are deciduous shrubs or vines. All varieties have tubular flowers which are mostly fragrant.

➤ *L. japonica,* Japanese Honeysuckle, 10 to 20 feet. An evergreen vine that can be a deciduous plant in colder areas of the United States. It is a quick-growing plant with a tendency to grow in many directions. Japanese honeysuckle will grow in many types of soils and is drought tolerant once established. Zone 4.

Miscanthus sinensis 'Variegatus'
Variegated Japanese Silver Grass
5 to 6 feet
Clumping white-and-green-striped, narrow-leaved ornamental grass. Striking on its own or foliage good for contrast with bright flowering plants. Has brushlike flower stalks in fall. Sun to partial shade. Zone 5.

Monarda didyma
Bee Balm, Oswego Tea
4 feet

Large, shrubby perennial native to New England, the East, and the upper Southeast. A member of the mint family (you can make a tea with bee balm). Can spread in the garden. Covered in late spring and summer with large, almost spiderlike blooms in scarlet shades. Leaves long, jagged, and dark green. Mildew can be a problem, but some of the new varieties are resistant. 'Cambridge Scarlet' and 'Croftway Pink' are popular selections. Attracts butterflies. Sun to part shade. Zone 4.

Monarda fistulosa
Wild Bergamont, Wild Bee Balm
2 to 3 feet

Smaller bee balm, with soft pink-lavender blooms. Native to East and Southeast, Texas. Sun to part shade.

Oenothera Berlandieri
Mexican Evening Primrose
To 12 inches

A perennial shrub with rose-pink cupped blossoms. Native to Texas and Mexico. It has good drought tolerance once established and requires little care. Full sun. Zone 2.

Oenothera missourensis
Ozark Sundrop, Yellow Evening Primrose
1 foot

Native from Central Plains down to Texas. Grows in low clumps, with

This pink cultivar of Wild Bee Balm (M. fistulosa) *is effectively grouped with purple coneflower (left) and silvery artemisia.*

buttercuplike flowers (in evening) of lemon yellow and dark green foliage. Needs sun, good drainage, but tolerates poor soils. Zone 5.

Pennisetum setaceum
Fountain Grass
3 to 4 feet

Another attractive ornamental grass, with very thin leaves and soft, plumelike flower heads. Varieties 'Atrosanguineum' and 'Rubrum' have purple grasses and flower plumes. Sun to partial shade. Zone 8.

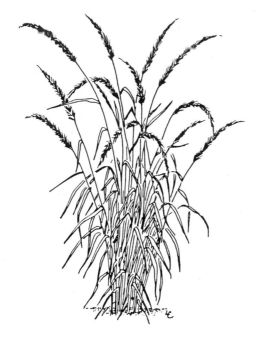

Fountain Grass.

Penstemon, or Beard Tongue.

Portulaca.

Penstemon spp.
Penstemon, Beard Tongue
Variable
These shrublike plants come from a
very large group of plants with showy
tubular flowers in many pastel colors.
They require full sun and need to be
planted in a well-draining soil. Most
species native to Northwest and West.
Zone 5.

Portulaca oleracea
Purslane
Perennial species, spreading low to the
ground, around 4 to 5 inches tall.
Small, succulentlike foliage and yellow
flowers. Sometimes considered a weed
because of its rapid growth, but it can
really take the heat of the South and
Southwest.

Rosa spp.
(See chapter on shrubs.)

Rudbeckia spp.
Black-eyed Susan
2 to 3 feet
A very popular garden plant, Black-eyed Susan works well in a cottage garden. Form is rounded clump. Bright yellow flowers with black centers, although some newer varieties have orange around the black center. Dark green foliage. *R. hirta* is more of a short-lived perennial. *R. fulgida* 'Goldsturm' has smaller blossoms. *Rudbeckias* are native American plants, in many regions.

Gray-green foliages make good partners for blue- or rose-hued plants. This Texas garden combines santolina and verbena effectively—almost as groundcovers.

William D. Adams

Salvia spp.
Sage
3 to 4 feet
There are hundreds of varieties of this shrublike perennial. Most of them have a strong scent. The flowers occur in spikelike clusters. Occurs in vivid indigo and purple shades, as well as red and white. Sage requires full sun. Many species are native to Texas and the South and Southwest. Zone 8.

SOME SAGE SELECTIONS

Botanical Name	Common Name	Height	Bloom Color
S. elegans	Pineapple Sage	2 feet	red
S. farinacea	Mealy Cup Sage	2 feet	indigo, purple
S. Greggii	Autumn Sage	2 to 3 feet	red
S. 'Indigo Spires'	—	1 to 2 feet	dark indigo
S. leucantha	Mexican Bush Sage	4 to 5 feet	light purple
S. officinalis	Culinary Sage	1 to 2 feet	blue, white

Santolina spp.
Santolina, Lavender Cotton
1 to 2 feet
A soft-looking, gray-green perennial/shrub with small pale yellow flowers. Grows in low, clumping mounds. Requires full sun and well-draining soil. *S. chamaecyparissus* works well in the West and South. Zone 7.

Saxifraga × *arendsii*
Rockfolis
An herbaceous perennial with a low-spreading habit. The flowers come in colors of red, rose, pink, and white. It requires full sun to partial shade. Zone 4.

Schizachryrium scoparium
Little Bluestem
3 to 5 feet
Attractive silver-blue (summer) ornamental grass that turns golden brown in the winter. Native to Plains, South, and parts of Southwest. Grows in more upright form than some of the other ornamental grasses. Good for a softer, more informal look in the garden.

Sedum **spp.**
Stonecrop, Sedum
Varies
These succulent perennials are often used as a groundcover or in rock gardens. Like many succulents, they are easy to root from cuttings and are fast-spreading plants. *S. telephium* 'Autumn Joy' is popular for its deep rose color and attracts butterflies. It requires full sun. Zone 7.

Solandra maxima
Cup of Gold Vine
Up to 40 feet
An evergreen vine from Mexico with 4- to 6-inch glossy leaves with yellow blooms. Normally this plant needs supports. Early spring blooms, the *maxima* makes a good seaside planting. Fair drought tolerance once it is established. A native of Mexico. Zone 8–9.

Verbena **spp.**
Verbena
1 to 2 feet
Cheery, low-mounding border plant, with lacy dark green foliage and ringed clusters of tiny blooms. Blooms come in many shades of pink, red, purple, scarlet, etc. Prefers sun and good drainage. May need occasional waterings during severe droughts. Zone 7–8.

CHOOSING A WATER SYSTEM

The most important factor in your water-thrifty garden, besides planting and design, is your choice of a watering system, its maintenance, and using the given water as efficiently as possible. In no other aspect of gardening has technology come into play so well as in watering and irrigation. With many of the new devices that have been developed, you can now be more efficient with the water for your shrubs, trees, groundcovers, lawns, and vines.

In water-thrifty gardening you must be water smart. That is, you must not allow your plants to become so dry that they decline and die, yet you can have a healthy landscape with economical use of water. And in many cases, you can wean plants from a heavy diet of fertilizer and water.

The amount of water a plant will need depends upon many factors. A small plant in a small container actually requires much more frequent watering than a larger, better established plant in your yard. Containers can only hold so much water and, during hot summer days, water is lost through evaporation, especially in clay containers where water is "wicked" out. In fact, a small bonsai often needs to be watered twice a day. The frequency can also be affected by temperature, humidity, and light. Wind is also a factor, causing *transpiration,* which is water loss through the leaves. This is one reason why, even though we may have more rain during the summer months, because of the high heat (and winds), we may still need to water more often than in the fall or winter.

Competition from larger trees and shrubs is an often overlooked factor. Competition is also one of the reasons that weed control is also an important factor in water conservation. (While Emerson said that a weed is simply a plant out of place, most gardeners feel differently when an aggressive, non-ornamental plant robs more valuable plants of their nutrients and water.)

WATERING

As I explained in the introduction, having a water-thrifty garden doesn't mean you never water at all. When you put in a drought-tolerant plant you can't simply forget to water it. Be observant of your new and existing plants: watch for the first indications of limp and slightly curled leaves that show a need for water (although if the leaves are very limp and very curled the plant is in serious trouble). You'll do better with longer waterings spaced farther apart than frequent short waterings. Watering your plants frequently and lightly doesn't encourage strong roots. Deep watering encourages roots, as they grow stronger by pushing to get more water. This is some of the principle behind drip watering systems (see below), which, instead of spraying water in general areas like traditional sprinkler systems do, concentrate drops in one area—by the plant—for a more thorough soak.

One other point we should make with watering is that if you water early in the day, you can avoid water loss through evaporation. The wind and sun will not cause rapid evaporation if the yard is watered well before the sun

comes up. Therefore, try to water as early as possible. Or, if you have a timer on your system, watering just about anytime after midnight will be helpful. It is also important to make sure that you are not wasting water by irrigating onto the sidewalk or driveway. So, adjust your watering system—whatever it is—so that water is only reaching your plants. Besides, an often overlooked drawback of excessive watering on concrete areas is that algae will grow on these areas, making a slippery, dangerous walking surface.

When you're ready to plan a new water system, or if you already have one, you will need to measure the water needed for your landscape, taking into account existing and new drought-tolerant plants and the zones they are in. With your present system check the amount of output. You can use rain gauges or even tuna cans throughout your yard, then turn on the system. After as little as 15 minutes, you can check the gauges or cans and measure how much water is going to the different areas of your yard. If you find a great difference between containers, then sprinkler heads or patterns need to be readjusted. Often something as simple as a clogged head can be the problem. You may want to try **moisture meters** for more accurate information on the watering efficiency of your system. **Soil probes** are also easy to use and by digging into the soil you can tell how well the water is trickling through your soil. The soil types mentioned in the soil improvement chapter can tell you the water-holding capacities of the soil you have to work with.

ZONES

The zones you planned for in chapter 1 come back into play here. Hopefully, you have now selected many new plants you need for your garden and assessed their watering needs. To review working in zones, Zone 1—the "oasis" area—represents plants with the most demanding water needs, with each subsequent zone representing diminishing needs until you reach a zone where the plants rely simply on your area's rainfall (after they've been established). Again, three simple zones should be sufficient, with Zone 2 for plants needing occasional waterings and Zone 3 for plants that can use the rainfall available. Because of their high water demands, though, turf areas are usually put in a zone of their own. Since Zone 1 has higher water demands, you need to plan your water system so that water is conveniently delivered there. For many gardeners, that may simply mean a system closer to the house, although, as you'll discover below, the new devices available mean that you may not have to lift a finger to get the watering done.

Knowing your area's typical rainfall (see map on page 00), the water needs of your present and new plants, and the

zones you've planned for your garden now prepares you to pick a water system.

THE DIFFERENT SYSTEMS

Today there are a great number of different systems for water delivery. One of them will be best suited for your landscape irrigation needs.

Many gardeners use a fixed system of rigid pipes with sprinkler heads attached on risers. Or, you may be using drip irrigation, using flexible plastic tubes, just underneath the mulch. Some people still use the simple system of dragging the garden hose, with sprinkler attached, to the area in need of water. If you do use hoses and sprinklers, you can select any number of different sprinkler heads. These include those that oscillate back and forth, rotary sprayers, those with bubblers, or even those which will emit water in a slow, soaking pattern along the length of the hose. Some will have fan heads or "impulse" heads, called a machine gun sprinkler. Some resemble a garden tractor that slowly moves along the length of the garden hose. These last, though, present problems of evaporation. Systems can be above ground or below. A below-ground system may seem complex to install, but they are increasingly made easy for gardeners. You can control patterns and amounts of water by selection of hoses, heads, pressure, and placement.

HOSES

If you are going to use the old-fashioned hose method, there are a number of materials that can be used. Hoses at one time were basically made from rubber, but now there are reinforced or unreinforced vinyl as well as fiber and cording systems. The old rubber hoses were rather dull in their appearance, heavy, only fairly flexible, and could be a problem as far as getting too cold to work with. Today, the reinforced vinyl hoses are more attractive, more flexible, and easier to work with in both cold and warm temperatures. Vinyl hoses should be protected from long-term exposure to hot sunlight.

Reinforced vinyl hoses are a good choice and are stronger than the unreinforced. Combinations of rubber and vinyl are usually the best of both. They are strong, flexible and seem to last longer. Diameter of the hose is measured by the size of the inside opening. This diameter can range from ½ inch, ⅝ inch, or ¾ inch. The difference in diameters may seem insignificant, but the larger the hose, even by a small amount, the more water will flow through it.

There are now many hose attachments that strictly regulate the flow of water. These water wands have switches at the base to stop and start the flow of water—so that no water is wasted in watering rounds. Heads on these attachments regulate the strength and type of flow, so that you can get a gentle stream or spray.

IMPACT SPRINKLERS

There are many different sprinkler heads that will give you a variety of patterns. Often they will be described as quarter, half, or whole circles. Of course there are heads for rectangular and square patterns. The typical sprinkler heads used to be all steel or brass. Now there are several combinations of metal and plastic heads. Although the plastic heads may be more easily broken, with proper care they can last a very long time. If you do use an impact head sprinkler, keep in mind they throw water thirty or forty feet. A small number of heads can give you a very large coverage area.

As alluded to above, the problem with this system is potential water loss through evaporation and runoff. Throwing the water such long distances means some gets on your yard and some doesn't. The percentages of water loss vary, but they can be substantial: up to 50% and 70% loss. Where water is scarce and/or rationed, it would be best to consider all possible water systems first. Still, there are innovations with this system that make it more worthwhile.

One of the first things I would tell you to do when choosing an impact sprinkler, pop-up, or bubbler is to plan your system by first laying it out on a piece of graph paper. You can look for your sprinklers to be pop-up heads (these are great as they are down below the grass or shrubs when not in use) or the impulse system I spoke about earlier. A combination of the two works well. You should be familiar with the buffers that can be used to keep sprinkler mist and spray from hitting areas you don't want watered. Many of the bubbler heads and/or gear driven sprinklers will be available through most irrigation outlets, hardware, or home improvement stores.

Often, the entire system will be laid out for you if you purchase all of your supplies from one retailer. Of course, besides designing your own system, there are always professional sprinkler system businesses that will design the perfect system for you, using a combination of equipment and types of heads. You will want to map out your property, in terms of walkways, decks, pools, etc., so that your irrigation will be as efficient and thrifty as possible.

If you do use a raised, automated system you should consider using automated electronic controllers. One of the greatest factors in this choice is that most of us are away from home at various times. With the automated system, the landscape gets watered regularly, even when we are not at home. Many suppliers and hardware stores will offer a variety of clocks or timers for the sprinkler system. Many are interesting, either very simple, like an old-fashioned clock, or fancy, like the minicomputers which can be programmed for a variety of days, times, and zones. Some systems have devices which will measure ground water availability and turn the system

on in time of need only. For example, the Tensiometer is a metal tube with a porous ceramic tip on one end and a pressure gauge on the other. Sensors that measure the amount of water in the device activate or do not activate the watering system, as the situation calls for. These are gaining popularity with the commercial landscaper.

One of the things to remember when installing your system is that you will have to replace broken sprinkler heads and risers from time to time. To repair a sprinkler head, you may have to dig down into the soil to fix the problem (especially if it is a broken riser, which is the tube coming off of the main pipe). Often you may find that a solvent cement was used to install the riser and you may have to take a hack saw and cut through the riser or main line in order to facilitate the repair. There are a number of keys and other devices that can be installed to make this sort of thing easier. Also, you may wish to take a fine wire to clean through the heads of your sprinklers from time to time to remove algae, sand, silt, or other materials which may clog the heads.

DRIP SYSTEMS

Probably the biggest irrigation improvement of the last decade has been in drip irrigation: water is applied directly where it is needed, to the root zone, through tiny spouts, or emitters—either above ground or below ground. It's

Emitters in a drip irrigation system, watering junipers being established as groundcover.

really a simple system that can help save in both material costs and in water conservation. In nurseries, an emitter is used to supply water to each container. The same theory works well in the home garden. Almost every nursery or home improvement store will have the tubing, fittings, and emitters for home garden use. They can be purchased in kits, or you can create your own system by purchasing needed parts and following the pattern of an existing system. Or instead, converter supplies will allow you to convert the existing system to drip irrigation. Where I have used drip systems, efficiency was increased as much as 50% to 60% higher than overhead sprinkling.

The benefits to the plants are something to consider as well: fewer disease problems due to water splashing on the foliage or heavy-watering sprinklers splashing up soil-borne diseases up onto the plant. With thorough, steady watering you avoid stressing the plant by making it languish between waterings. Since the emitters drip only on the plants you want, weeds miss out and are reduced.

A drip irrigation system is usually composed of flexible tubing ½ inch diameter or less with periodic smaller tubes (¼ inch diameter) branching off (emitters) that provide the drips. The versatility this kind of system allows means that you can make it conform to the zones you've set up—and you can even use drip spouts to take care of any container plants you have. Connect the tubing to make the system as long or short as you need. A pressure regulator does what its name indicates— keeping the water pressure at a manageable level for the drip spouts. It helps to know the kind of soil you have and about how fast it drains (see chapter 2) so that you can regulate the flow you'll need. The drip irrigation system will need to be flushed periodically, and will need filters to keep it clean of residue. It is also possible to get components that will apply fertilizer—yet another labor-saving device. As mentioned above with the sprinkler systems, timers now enable the gardener to not even have to turn on the water faucet. There are solar timers and timers that respond to your garden's water needs.

Most irrigation system companies supply detailed booklets on planning your water systems—some will even do it for you. The booklets are handy to figure out lengths of tubing and accessories. The installation procedures are similar to that of the sprinkler system above and for soaker hoses below:

1. Draw your house, garage, driveway, walks and outbuildings to scale on graph paper.

2. Add existing trees, hedges, etc.

3. Add in any new plantings you have in mind, incorporating the zones that you have created for a water-thrifty plan.

4. Mark location of your water supply—faucets or well pump, if applicable.

5. Decide what system or combination of systems suits your garden. Draw in roughly the system(s) lines you need, keeping everything to scale so that you know the lengths needed.

6. Note on your plan as best you can the materials needed from the supplier's booklet, or, if you don't have a booklet, what you now have drawn is probably enough to take to a hardware or gardening supply store to get supplies.

Once you get all your supplies and assemble the tubing—except pressure regulators and ends of hoses or tubing— hook the system up to the faucet and run the water full force for several minutes in order to dislodge any debris that might have entered the lines during assembly. Then add the pressure regulators and close the ends of the tubing. With your system finished, turn the faucet on again and let the system run for 10 to 15 minutes, checking all connections and checking for leaks. When the system checks out, you can cover with mulch or bury the tubing as you desire. (The system you choose may have different requirements, so always be sure to read the manufacturer's instructions carefully.)

SOAKER HOSES

Soaker hoses operate on the same principle as drip irrigation systems, delivering

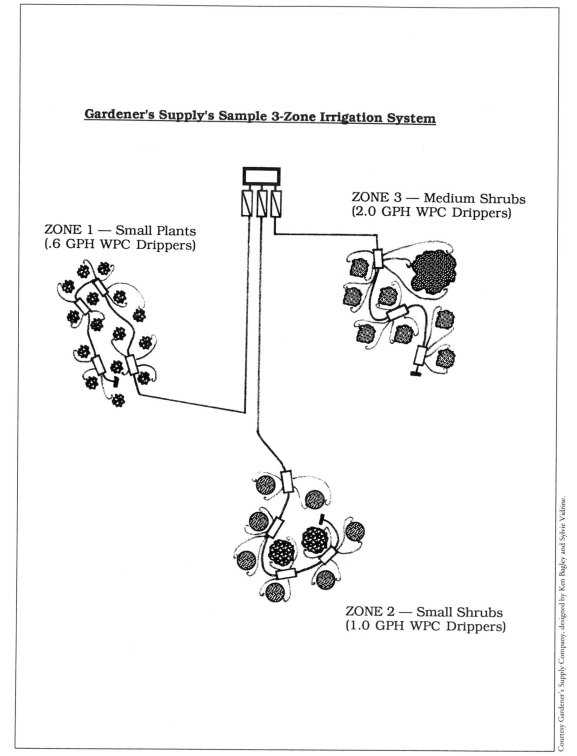

Gardener's Supply's Sample 3-Zone Irrigation System

ZONE 3 — Medium Shrubs
(2.0 GPH WPC Drippers)

ZONE 1 — Small Plants
(.6 GPH WPC Drippers)

ZONE 2 — Small Shrubs
(1.0 GPH WPC Drippers)

Courtesy Gardener's Supply Company, designed by Ken Bagley and Sylvie Vidrine.

Most irrigation/sprinkler companies will help you create an irrigation plan—or simply do one for your garden. Here is an example.

slow, thorough watering in an efficient, controlled manner. The hoses either "leak" or "sweat" the moisture along their length through tiny openings. Installation can be as simple as attachment to an outside water faucet. It's easy, then, to snake your soaker hose through flower beds and other plantings. As with drip systems, since soaker hoses are putting water directly at the thirsty roots, you avoid fungus problems caused when plant foliage gets wet. Most soaker hoses are inconspicuously dark. You can leave them above ground, put them below ground, or cover them with a layer of mulch. Below ground, you avoid evaporation and ensure even water distribution. Once set in place, you can forget them and not have to worry about accidental damage you might have with dragging around a regular hose.

A system I find effective is Moisture Master. This system can be used in the greenhouse, nursery, vegetable garden, and for trees and shrubs in the landscape. Water "weeps" uniformly from one end to the other. It kept the plants' roots moist but not overwet. Fewer weeds cropped up because water wasn't sprayed over the entire bed, just delivered to the desired plants. Another plus with this system is that it is made from recycled rubber—old tires. This system takes about 700,000 old tires out of the environment. The tubing is created by mixing polyethylene with the recycled rubber. Moisture Master claims to save

in water costs by about as much as 70 percent, and is easy to install and maintain.

I also found Moisture Master effective along narrow strips, along the sides of houses and walkways. Conventional systems may discolor sidewalks, fences, and the sides of houses with iron and other mineral deposits in the water.

GRAY WATER

"Gray Water" is a good idea that is actually an old idea—recycling or reclaiming used water. With a federal grant, St. Petersburg, Florida ran a successful experiment where treated sewage water was filtered to be used again in the landscape. They discovered that they could reuse a majority of the water—and that there was no increase in the use of potable water. While many cities and towns will start investigating water reclamation, you can use home water in the landscape, too. (Check with your city, however, not all communities allow gray water use yet.) This water includes that from the bath, sink, washer, dishwasher (not toilet water)—taking care to avoid cleaners with ammonia or chlorine. And it's fairly uncomplicated to hook up pipes from the inside to the outside, and then filter the water, often through a series of small troughs. Use gray water on your ornamental plantings—not on vegetable gardens.

RAIN BARRELS

Another old-fashioned and simple idea is saving rain water. Cisterns that collected rain water used to be a common feature in yesterday's yards. It's still easy to do on a smaller scale for today's small garden. Simply connect your downspouts from roof gutters to a drumlike rain barrel. They're usually constructed of tough plastic and come with a tap on the end. A filter and/or screen on the top of the barrel keeps out leaves, twigs, and mosquito larvae (a very important concern when you have standing water). Attaching a hose to the barrel's tap allows you to water the garden. Many garden supply stores and water system companies offer rain barrels; the Gardener's Supply Company listed in the Appendix is one example. Some areas' rainfall amounts may not make this idea practical, but saving rain water is one economical way to take care of your garden's water needs.

MAINTAINING THE WATER-THRIFTY GARDEN

Maintaining the water-thrifty landscape is important. Even the best designed landscape can look rather unkept in as little as three to six months if it is not maintained properly. Yet often, gardeners tend to over-fertilize, over-water, and over-prune in the traditional landscape. While a water-thoughtful landscape is not maintenance-free, these tasks don't have to be labor-intensive.

USING FERTILIZERS

Most nurserymen are growing specific plants and consequently use a high nitrogen fertilizer. In a low-water-use-type of landscape, however, use a low-nitrogen fertilizer. Nitrogen promotes *rapid* growth—not what you want. I recommend a 5-10-10 or a 2-10-10 ratio in fertilizing, or any other low-nitrogen fertilizer. (The percentages in the ratio represent nitrogen, phosphorus, and potassium, respectively.) By using a high nitrogen fertilizer, you promote new growth that requires additional watering. Where water conservation is paramount, consider fertilizing in a maintenance mode. As the proverb says, "Moderation is the key." Fertilizing is a good example of this axiom.

The form of the fertilizer you use can vary, liquid, granular, or time-released. Each would have an appropriate application in your particular landscape. I recommend a combination of the three, and I use liquids as "a shot in the arm" to pop growth in plants. In many cases, use a time-released fertilizer like Osmoscoate, along with some natural organics, which are usually low in their analysis, such as 2-2-2 or 1-1-1, and some water-soluble fertilizers—which give longer results, especially in the spring or summer.

PRUNING PLANTS PROPERLY

You don't have to get out the hedge clippers every week—really. In your new garden, you don't have to prune as much as you would in a traditional garden. Trimming a lot of the foliage allows more sunlight to get through, and therefore dries out the plant more quickly. Trimming out heavy branches allows sun in that may increase the risk of sunburn to the plant. During drought or times of water rationing, you don't want to prune the plant, since its root system has already grown large enough to support the plant at that size. Pruning stimulates growth, growth which will then require additional water. Therefore, during dry times, pruning should be reduced.

Once your landscape is established you will have to do some maintenance pruning. Of course, if you select the proper plant for its suited location, pruning will not be necessary. Use plants with more of a "free" form, such as native hollies, cenizos and other native plants. These shrubs and plants grow as they will—as they would in na-

ture—avoiding the constant trimming into formal boxes. With these looser, more natural shapes, pruning becomes an occasional matter. "Natural" and open shrubs also give insects fewer areas to hide, yet are more inviting to wildlife than formal, rigidly clipped hedges.

Prune dead twigs or branches; these do nothing for the plant. Branches that are rubbing against each other should be trimmed. Any severely diseased or insect-damaged parts of plants must be trimmed out and removed. Pruning helps rejuvenate an older shrub that no longer flowers. In special cases where pruning is needed, if you trim off a terminal bud, lateral branches will sprout. This happens because hormones that keep these lateral buds in check are reduced by cutting the terminal buds off.

Of course, many plants will eventually send up long shoots; nurserymen call this getting "leggy." That leggy growth needs to be removed. But remember when trimming that you will encourage more branches to sprout. If the plant starts to look too straggly, trim it back about a third to a half of its original height. In most landscapes, plants at two, three, or even four feet can look balanced with the rest of the original landscaping. If, on the other hand, the shrub gets *too* large, where you can't locate your windows or doors, the plant needs to be trimmed or even replaced with a more suitable plant.

With shrubs and hedges, keep the bottom wider than the top. This general shaping allows more sunlight to the sides, keeps the plant healthy and symmetrical, and keeps leaves throughout the hedge and not just at the top.

When you prune, start clean. Keep your tools clean, dipping them in a bleach/water solution between cuts to avoid spreading disease. Keep your tools sharp as well, to make a nice cut—normally a slanted cut, at about a 45° angle, and above the bud. When you do this, the limb will branch out in the direction of the bud.

MANAGING YOUR MOWER

One of the keys to maintaining a dry landscape is mowing correctly. Use the proper lawn mower for your lawn area. You may need a reel mower for fine grasses such as Zoysia or Bermuda or some of the northern mixtures, but, for many other grasses, a rotary blade will be adequate.

You need to mow on a regular basis. One important reason for mowing consistently is weed control. As we have discussed, weeds are in direct competition for water with the preferred plantings in your yard. Also, if you let the grass get too long between mowings, it will often be a shock to the grass, shortly turning it brown.

Mow so that no more than 1/3 of the height of the blade is removed at any one cutting. Yes, it is true that blue grass, in the north, can be mowed at 2 inches, or that on a golf green you can mow at 3/16 inches, but, in general, the lower you cut the lawn, the more water it will require. The taller the blade of grass, the deeper and stronger the root system—and a healthy root system pulls in the nutrients. Taller blades provide shade to the lower portion of the grass.

An important safety tip: **Do NOT cut the grass when it is wet.** Wet grass is difficult to cut, and it is easy for the gardener to lose footing and slip into the mower, sometimes with tragic results. Take care also to avoid bumping the mower into the trees and shrubs. Such bumping can cause permanent damage to the plant. It is best to keep grass away with a mulch, or to put a protective cover around the base of the plant.

Mulching mowers and mulching blades are new devices that have swept the country in recent years. This concept is a good one, and I recommend that you leave the clippings on your lawn. Clippings provide nutrients and shade to the lawn. (You should not, however, leave the clippings if you mow your summer home lawn only every six months or so—then I would definitely rake up the hay field afterwards!)

It has been said before, but bears repeating: the mower blade must be kept sharp. A dull blade can and will kill a lawn by chewing up the grass blades rather than cleanly cutting them off. A dull blade can damage a lawn more readily than common insects and diseases.

WEEDING AND WEED CONTROL

Weeding and weed control is an inevitable factor in a water-thrifty landscape. When we try to be as conservative as we can with water, we must first realize that any plant out of place can be called a weed, because it is using water and nutrients intended for other plants. Birds, the wind, and even people are guilty of dropping weed seeds in unwanted areas. Weed seeds travel in birds' feathers, drift in the wind, and adhere to pants legs and dog and cat fur.

Common ways of removing weeds include hand picking. This simply means to dig up the weeds, either with bare hands or with a scuffle hoe or Roto-tiller. Normally this is done prior to planting. Then, of course, either mulching materials or landscape fabric can be used to block the weeds.

Many people prefer herbicides. Herbicides are chemicals that kill plants and can do a good job on your weeds. But if you use herbicides, you MUST read and follow the label directions carefully. Any herbicide that kills weeds will just as easily damage and kill your desired plants as well. Used carefully and correctly, I have found herbicides to be very effective.

Weed killers are usually divided into two categories, pre-emergence and post-emergence products. Pre-emergence herbicides kill the weed seed before it sprouts. To be effective, most of these must be applied before germination. In some cases pre-emergence herbicides in lawns must be used over a period of months or years to be effective. The post-emergence herbicides eliminate weeds that have germinated and are actively growing. Many of these products have been developed to control weeds in lawns and planting beds. Of course they can be effective especially on noxious weeds, such as poison ivy. All weeds should be sprayed when there is little wind, to avoid the mist of the herbicide blowing to preferred plants that may be damaged by the chemical.

Glyphosate is a product that is quite effective and safe if used according to directions. Used in weedy areas, it is taken into the chlorophyll of the plant and into the root of the plant to kill it. It ties up to the soil particles quickly and it is safe to plant the soil again shortly after use of this product. Glyphosate is sold under the trade names of Round-Up®, Kleen-Up®, or Kills All®.

It is always a good idea to label sprayers used only for weeds. Herbicide residue can remain in the sprayer and damage plants even when another product is used later on.

Resources

CROSS REFERENCE OF LANDSCAPE PLANTS

What follows are plant selections for the various regions of the United States. Once you find a plant listed for your region, check back to the chapter description to be sure that it's in your zone, since each region may have several hardiness zones.

THE PACIFIC NORTHWEST/NORTHWEST

TREES
Aesculus californica, California Buckeye
Albizia julibrissin, Mimosa
Alnus rhombifolia, White Alder
Arbutus Unedo, Strawberry Tree
Broussonetia papyrifera, Paper Mulberry
Cedrus atlantica, Atlas Cedar
Cedrus Deodara, Deodar Cedar
Celtis occidentalis, Common Hackberry
Celtis reticulata, Western Hackberry
Cercis canadensis, Eastern Redbud
Cercis occidentalis, Western Redbud
Elaeagnus angustifolia, Russian Olive
Ficus carica, Edible Fig
Juglans hindsii, California Black Walnut

Koelreuteria formosana, Golden Raintree
Ligustrum japanicum, Japanese Privet
Pinus canariensis, Canary Island Pine
Pinus roxburghii, Chir Pine
Pinus thunbergiana, Japanese Black Pine
Quercus ilex, Holly Oak
Quercus macrocarpa, Bur Oak
Quercus palustris, Pin Oak
Robinia spp., Locust

SHRUBS AND PERENNIALS
Achillea filipendulina, Fern-leaf Yarrow
Achillea millefolium, Common Yarrow
Alyssum saxatilis, Alyssum
Antennaria rosea, Cat's Foot
Arctostaphylos Uva-ursi 'Point Reyes Kinnikinick,' Kinnikinick
Artemisia spp., Artemisia
Artemisia ludoviciana, Silver King Artemisia
Aster spp., Aster
Atriplex canescens, Four-wing Saltbush
Baptisia australis, False Indigo
Caragana spp., Pea Shrub
Ceanothus spp., Wild Lilac
Cerastium tomentosum, Snow-in-the-Summer
Coreopsis grandiflora, Coreopsis
Cotoneaster apiculatus, Cranberry Cotoneaster

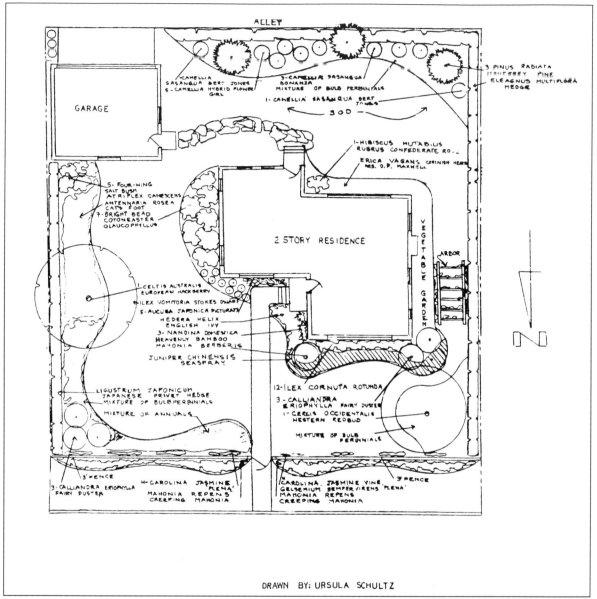

The Pacific Northwest.

Cotoneaster congestus 'Likiang'	*Genista* spp., Broom
Cotoneaster Dammeri	*Helleborus foetidus*
Cotoneaster divaricatus	*Helleborus lividus corsicus,* Corsican
Cotoneaster horizontalis, Rock Cotoneaster	Hellebore
Cotoneaster salicifolius, Carpet Cotoneaster	*Hemerocallis* spp., Day Lily
Elaeagnus multiflora, Cherry Elaeagnus	*Iris* spp., Bearded Iris
Gaillardia grandiflora, Blanketflower	*Juniperus conferta* 'Blue Pacific'

Juniperus horizontalis
Lavandula angustifolia, English Lavender
Lavandula stoechas, Spanish Lavender
Liatris spicata, Gayfeather
Mahonia aquifolium, Oregon Grape
Mahonia repens, Creeping Mahonia
Monarda didyma, Bee Balm
Oenothera Berlandieri, Mexican Evening
   Primrose
Pennisetum setaceum, Fountain Grass
Pyracantha spp., Firethorn
Rudbeckia spp., Black Eyed Susan
Saxifraga × arendsii, Rockfolis
Sedum telephium 'Autumn Joy,' Stonecrop
Taxus spp., Yew
Verbena spp., Verbena

CALIFORNIA

TREES

Acacia spp., Acacia
Aesculus californica, California Buckeye
Albizia julibrissin, Mimosa
Alnus rhombifolia, White Alder
Arbutus Unedo, Strawberry Tree
Caesalpinia spp., Bird-of-Paradise
Casuarina spp., Australian Pine
Cedrus atlantica, Atlas Cedar
Cedrus Deodora, Deodar Cedar
Cedrus australis, European Hackberry
Celtis reticulata, Western Hackberry
Ceratonia siliqua, St. John's Bread
Cercis occidentalis, Western Redbud
Chilopsis linearis, Desert Willow
Cinnamomum camphora, Camphor Tree
Cupressus sempervirens, Italian Cypress
Eucalyptus spp., Eucalyptus

Ficus carica, Edible Fig
Ginkgo biloba, Maidenhair Tree
Grevillea robusta, Silk Oak Tree
Grevillea 'Noellii'
Hakea spp.
Juglans californica, California Walnut
Juglans Hindsii, California Black Walnut
Koelreuteria formosana, Golden Raintree
Lagerstroemia indica, Crape Myrtle
Laurus nobilis, Sweet Bay
Liquidambar styraciflua, Sweet Gum
Olea europaea, Common Olive Tree
Parkinsonia aculeata, Jerusalem Thorn
Pinus canariensis, Canary Island Pine
Pinus eldarica, Eldarica Pine
Pinus halepensis, Aleppo Pine
Pinus radiata, Monterey pine
Pinus thunbergiana, Japanese Black Pine
Prosopis glandulosa Torreyana, Mesquite
Prunus ilicifolia, Holly-leaf Cherry
Quercus agrifolia, Coast Live Oak
Quercus ilex, Holly Oak
Quercus suber, Cork Oak
Robinia spp., Locust
Schinus molle, California Pepper Tree

SHRUBS AND PERENNIALS

Acanthus mollis, Acanthus
Achillea millefolium, Common Yarrow
Aesculus californica, California Buckeye
Agapanthus africanus, Lily of the Nile
Agave americana, Century Plant
Aloe spp., Aloe
Alyogyne huegelii, Blue Hibiscus
Alyssum saxatilis, Alyssum
Antennaria rosea, Cat's Foot
Arctostaphylos manzanita, Manzanita
Artemisia spp., Artemisia
Artemisia ludoviciana, Silver King Artemisia

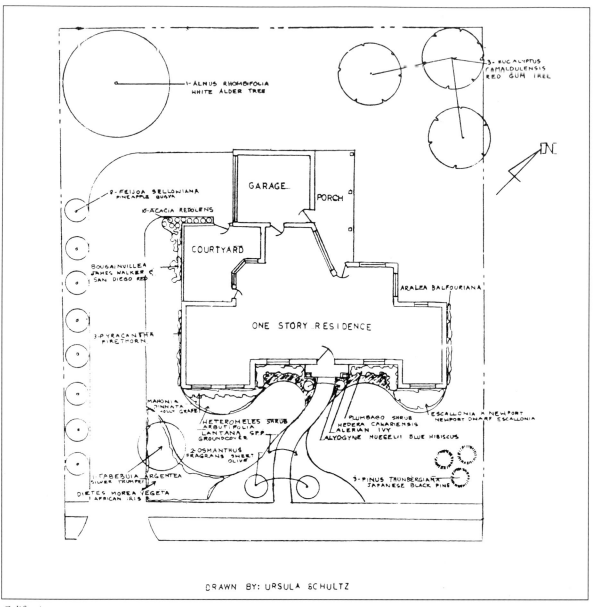

California.

Aster spp., Aster

Atriplex canescens, Four-wing Saltbush

Baccharis pilularis, Coyote Bush

Bougainvillea spp., Bougainvillea

Caesalpinia pulcherrima, Barbados Pride

Calliandra eriophylla, Fairy Duster

Canna × generalis, Canna

Cassia artemisioides, Feathery Cassia

Ceanothus spp., Wild Lilac

Cerastium tomentosum,
   Snow-in-the-Summer

Cistus spp., Rock Rose

Coreopsis grandiflora, Coreopsis

Correa × 'Dusley Bell's,' Australian Fuchsia

Cotoneaster spp., Cotoneaster

Cytisus, Broom Shrub

Delosperma Cooperi, Ice Plant

Dietes vegeta, Butterfly Iris

Erigeron Karvinskianus, Santa Barbara Daisy

Eriogonum spp., Ornamental Buckwheat

Escallonia spp., Escallonia

Eschscholzia californica, California Poppy

Gaillardia grandiflora, Blanketflower

Hamelia patens, Firebush

Heteromeles arbutifolia

Hibiscus rosa sinensis, Chinese Hibiscus

Iris spp., Bearded Iris

Lagerstroemia indica, Crape Myrtle

Lantana spp., Lantana

Lavandula spp., Lavender

Mahonia pinnata, California Holly Grape

Mahonia repens, Creeping Mahonia

Miscanthus sinensis 'Variegatus,' Variegated
  Japanese Silver Grass

Nerium Oleander, Oleander

Pavonia spp., Rock Rose

Pennisetum setaceum, Fountain Grass

Penstemon spp., Beard Tongue

Portulaca oleracea, Purslane

Pyracantha spp., Firethorn

Rhapiolepis indica, India Hawthorn

Rosa 'Don Juan'

Rosmarinus officinalis, Rosemary

Rudbeckia spp., Black-Eyed Susan

Salvia spp., Sage

Santolina spp., Lavender Cotton

Scaevola × 'Mauve Clusters'

Taxus spp., Yew

Verbena spp., Verbena

Yucca spp., Yucca

THE SOUTHWEST

TREES

Acacia spp., Acacia

Acer grandidentatum, Bigtooth Maple

Caesalpinia spp., Bird-of-Paradise

Casuarina spp., Australian Pine

Celtis pallida, Desert Hackberry

Celtis reticulata, Western Hackberry

Ceratonia siliqua, St. John's Bread

Cercidium floridum, Palo Verde

Chilopsis linearis, Desert Willow

Cupressus arizonica, Arizona Cypress

Cupressus glabra, Arizona Smooth-Bark
  Cypress

Eucalyptus spp., Eucalyptus

Fraxinus velutina, Arizona Ash

Juglans californica, California Walnut

Juglans major, Arizona Walnut

Parkinsonia aculeata, Jerusalem Thorn

Prosopis glandulosa Torreyana, Mesquite

Prosopis velutina, Arizona Mesquite

Rhus glabra, Smooth Sumac

Rhus ovata, Sugarbush

SHRUBS AND PERENNIALS

Agave americana, Century Plant

Agave victoriae-reginae, Queen Victoria
  Maguey

Aloe spp., Aloe

Artemisia ludoviciana, Silver King Artemisia

Atriplex lentiformis, Quail Bush

Berberis trifoliata, Agarita

Cacti spp., Cactus

Caesalpinia gilliesii, Bird-of-Paradise

Calliandra eriophylla, Fairy Duster

Cassia spp.

Cotoneaster spp., Cotoneaster

Dodonaea viscosa, Hopseed Bush

Eriogonum spp., Ornamental Buckwheat
Eschscholzia californica, California Poppy
Gaillardia grandiflora, Blanketflower
Hesperaloe parviflora, Red Yucca
Lantana montividensis, Lavender Lantana
Leucophyllum frutescens, Cenizo
Nerium Oleander, Oleander
Oenothera Berlandiari, Mexican Evening
　　Primrose
Pavonia spp., Rock Rose
Portulaca oleracea, Purslane
Rosa banksia, Lady Banks' Rose
Rosmarinus officinalis, Rosemary
Salvia spp., Sage
Santolina spp., Lavender Cotton
Yucca spp., Yucca

THE ROCKY MOUNTAINS

TREES
Acer Ginnala, Amur Maple
Acer glabrum, Rocky Mountain Maple
Acer grandidentatum, Bigtooth Maple
Alnus rhombifolia, White Alder
Caragana, Pea Shrub
Catalpa speciosa, Catalpa
Celtis occidentalis, Common Hackberry
Elaeagnus angustifolia, Russian Olive
Fraxinus pennsylvanica, Green Ash
Koelreuteria formosana, Golden Raintree
Olea europaea, Common Olive Tree
Quercus macrocarpa, Bur Oak
Rhus glabra, Smooth Sumac
Robinia spp., Locust

SHRUBS AND PERENNIALS
Achillea millefolium, Common Yarrow

Alyssum saxatilis, Alyssum
Aquilegia spp., Columbine
Arctostaphylos Uva-ursi 'Point Reyes
　　Kinnikinick,' Kinnikinick
Artemisia absinthium, Common Wormwood
Artemisia ludoviciana, Silver King Artemisia
Aster spp., Aster
Atriplex canescens, Four-wing Saltbush
Berberis × *mentorensis*, Mentor Barberry
Berberis thunbergii 'autropurpurea,' Red
　　Leaf Barberry
Berberis thunbergii 'Crimson Pygmy,'
　　Crimson Pygmy Barberry
Caragana spp., Pea Shrub
Caryopteris × *clandonensis*, Blue Mist
Cerastium tomentosum, Snow-in-the-
　　Summer
Chaenomeles japonica 'Minerva,' Flowering
　　Quince
Coreopsis grandiflora, Coreopsis
Cotoneaster apiculatus, Cranberry
　　Cotoneaster
Cotoneaster divaricatus
Cotoneaster horizontalis, Rock Cotoneaster
Echinops exaltatus, Globe Thistle
Elaeagnus multiflora, Cherry Elaeagnus
Gaillardia grandiflora, Blanketflower
Hedera helix, English Ivy
Ilex spp., Holly
Iris spp., Bearded Iris
Juniperus chinensis 'San Jose'
Juniperus horizontalis 'Bar Harbor'
Juniperus horizontalis 'Prince of Wales'
Juniperus horizontalis 'Wiltonii,' Blue Rug
　　Juniper
Juniperus × *media* 'Hetzi'
Juniperus × *media Pfitzeriana*, Green Pfitzer
　　Juniper

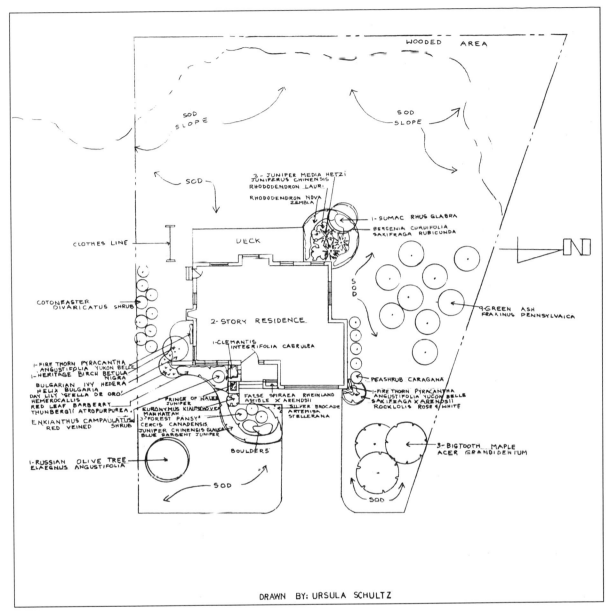

WOODED AREA

SOD SLOPE

SOD SLOPE

SOD

3- JUNIPER MEDIA HETZI
JUNIPERUS CHINENSIS
RHODODENDRON LAURI
RHODODENDRON NOVA ZEMBLA

1- SUMAC RHUS GLABRA
BERGENIA CURDIFOLIA
SAXIFRAGA RUBICUNDA

CLOTHES LINE

DECK

COTONEASTER
DIVARICATUS SHRUB

SOD

2- STORY RESIDENCE

9-GREEN ASH
FRAXINUS PENNSYLVAICA

1-CLEMANTIS
INTEGRIFOLIA CAERULEA

1-FIRE THORN PYRACANTHA
ANGUSTIFOLIA YUKON BELLE
1-HERITAGE BIRCH BETULA NIGRA

BULGARIAN IVY HEDERA
HELIX BULGARIA
DAY LILY 'STELLA DE ORO'
HEMEROCALLIS
RED LEAF BARBERRY
THUNBERGII ATROPURPUREA

ENKIANTHUS CAMPAULATUS
RED VEINED   SHRUB

PRINCE OF WALES
JUNIPER
EURONYMUS KIAUTSCHOVEA
MAN HATTAN
3-FOREST PANSY'
CERCIS CANADENSIS
JUNIPER CHINENSIS GLAUCA
BLUE BARBENT JUNIPER

FALSE SPIRAEA RHEINLAND
ASTILBE X ARENDSII

SILVER BROCADE
ARTEMISA
STELLERANA

PEASHRUB CARAGANA

1-FIRE THORN PYRACANTHA
ANGUSTIFOLIA YUCON BELLE
SAXIFRAGA X ARENDSII
ROCKLOLIS ROSE &/WHITE

1-RUSSIAN OLIVE TREE
ELAEGNUS ANGUSTIFOLIA

BOULDERS

SOD

3-BIGTOOTH MAPLE
ACER GRANDIDENTUM

SOD

DRAWN BY: URSULA SCHULTZ

The Rocky Mountains.

Juniperus × media Pfitzeriana glauca, Blue Pfitzer

Lavandula angustifolia, English Lavender

Liatris spicata, Gayfeather

Lonicera japonica, Japanese Honeysuckle

Mahonia aquifolium, Oregon Grape

Mahonia repens, Creeping Mahonia

Pyracantha spp., Firethorn

Rhus glabra, Smooth Sumac

Rudbeckia spp., Black-Eyed Susan

Santolina spp., Lavender Cotton

Schizachryrium scoparium, Little Bluestem

Sedum spp., Stonecrop

Yucca spp., Yucca

THE MIDWEST AND CENTRAL PLAINS

TREES
Acer Ginnala, Amur Maple
Acer palmatum, Japanese Maple
Acer rubrum, Red Maple
Caragana, Pea Shrub
Catalpa speciosa, Catalpa
Cedrus atlantica, Atlas Cedar
Celtis laevigata, Mississippi Hackberry
Celtis occidentalis, Common Hackberry
Cercis canadensis, Eastern Redbud
Elaeagnus angustifolia, Russian olive
Fraxinus pennsylvanica, Green Ash
Ginkgo biloba, Maidenhair Tree
Gymnocladus dioica, Coffee Tree
Ilex decidua, Possumhaw Holly
Ilex opaca, American Holly
Koelreuteria formosana, Golden Raintree
Ligustrum japonicum, Japanese Privet
Liquidambar styraciflua, Sweet Gum
Pinus thunbergiana, Japanese Black Pine
Quercus macrocarpa, Bur Oak
Quercus palustris, Pin Oak
Rhus glabra, Smooth Sumac
Robinia spp., Locust

Shrubs and Perennials
Abelia × grandiflora, Glossy Abelia
Achillea millefolium, Common Yarrow
Alyssum saxatilis, Alyssum
Aquilegia spp., Columbine
Artemisia ludoviciana, Silver King Artemisia
Aster spp., Aster
Atriplex canescens, Four-wing Saltbush
Berberis × mentorensis, Mentor Barberry
Berberis thunbergii 'atropurpea,' Red Leaf
   Barberry

Berberis thunbergii 'Aurea,' Yellow Leaf
   Barberry
Berberis thunbergii 'Crimson Pygmy'
Cerastium tomentosum, Snow-in-the-
   Summer
Chaenomeles japonica 'Minerva,' Flowering
   Quince
Chrysanthemum morifolium,
   Chrysanthemum
Coreopsis grandiflora, Coreopsis
Coreopsis verticillata 'Moonbeam'
Cotoneaster apiculatus, Cranberry
   Cotoneaster
Cotoneaster Dammeri
Cotoneaster divaricatus
Echinacea purpurea, Purple Coneflower
Echinops exaltatus, Globe Thistle
Gaillardia grandiflora, Blanketflower
Hedera helix, English Ivy
Helianthus Maximiliani, Maximilian
   Sunflower
Helianthus salicifolius
Hemerocallis spp., Day Lily
Ilex cornuta 'Burfordii,' Burford Holly
Ilex × 'Nellie R. Stevens'
Iris spp., Bearded Iris
Juniperus chinensis 'San Jose'
Juniperus horizontalis 'Bar Harbor'
Juniperus horizontalis 'Wiltonii,' Blue Rug
   Juniper
Juniperus × media 'Hetzi'
Lavandula angustifolia, English Lavender
Liatris spicata, Gayfeather
Mahonia aquifolium, Oregon Grape
Monarda didyma, Bee Balm
Oenothera missourensis, Ozark Sundrop
Pyracantha spp., Firethorn
Rudbeckia spp., Black-Eyed Susan
Saxifraga × arendsii, Rockfolis

Schizachryrium scoparium, Little Bluestem
Taxus spp., Yew

TEXAS

TREES

Acacia spp., Acacia
Acer grandidentatum, Bigtooth Maple
Caesalpinia spp., Bird-of-Paradise
Catalpa speciosa, Catalpa
Cedrus Deodara, Deodar Cedar
Celtis laevigata, Mississippi Hackberry
Cercidum floridum, Palo Verde
Cercis canadensis, Redbud
Chilopsis linearis, Desert Willow
Cornus florida, Flowering Dogwood
Cupressus arizonica, Arizona Cypress
Feijoa sellowiana, Pineapple Guava
Ficus carica, Edible Fig
Ilex decidua, Possumhaw Holly
Ilex vomitoria, Yaupon Holly
Koelreuteria formosana, Golden Raintree
Lagerstroemia indica, Crape Myrtle
Laurus nobilis, Sweet Bay
Liquidambar styraciflua, Sweet Gum
Magnolia grandiflora, Southern Magnolia
Myrica cerifera, Wax Myrtle
Parkinsonia aculeata, Jerusalem Thorn
Pinus elliotti, Slash Pine
Prosopis spp., Mesquite
Prunus caroliniana, Cherry Laurel
Quercus macrocarpa, Bur Oak
Quercus palustris, Pin Oak
Quercus shumardii, Shumard Red Oak
Quercus stellata, Post Oak
Quercus virginiana, Live Oak
Rhus glabra, Smooth Sumac
Rhus ovata, Sugarbush

Robinia spp., Locust
Washingtonia robusta, Washington Palm

SHRUBS AND PERENNIALS

Achillea millefolium, Common Yarrow
Agapanthus africanus, Lily of the Nile
Agave americana, Century Plant
Agave victoriae-reginae, Queen Victoria
    Maguey
Aloe spp., Aloe
Alyssum saxatilis, Alyssum
Antigonon leptopus, Coral Vine
Aquilegia canadensis, Wild Columbine
Artemisia ludoviciana, Silver King Artemisia
Asparagus densiflorus
Aster spp., Aster
Atriplex canescens, Four-wing Saltbush
Baptisia australis, False Indigo
Berberis trifoliata, Agarita
Bougainvillea spp., Bougainvillea
Caesalpinia pulcherrima, Barbados Pride
Caladium spp., Caladium
Calliandra eriophylla, Fairy Duster
Campsis radicans, Trumpet Creeper
Canna × *generalis,* Canna
Cassia corymbosa, Flowery Senna
Cistus spp., Rock Rose
Clematis paniculata, Sweet Autumn Clematis
Clytostoma callistegioides, Lavender Trumpet
    Vine
Convolvulus spp., Morning Glory
Coreopsis verticillata 'Moonbeam'
Cotoneaster spp., Cotoneaster
Cytisus spp., Broom Shrub
Delosperma Cooperi, Ice Plant
Distictis buccinatoria, Scarlet Trumpet Vine
Echinacea purpurea, Purple Coneflower
Eschscholzia californica, California Poppy
Gaillardia grandiflora, Blanketflower

Gelsimium sempervirens, Carolina Jasmine
Hamelia patens, Firebush
Helianthus Maximiliani, Maximilian Sunflower
Helianthus salicifolius
Hemerocallis spp., Day Lily
Hesperaloe parviflora, Red Yucca
Hibiscus rosa-sinensis, Chinese Hibiscus
Ilex cornuta 'Burfordii,' Burford Holly
Ilex cornuta 'Rotunda,' Dwarf Chinese Holly
Ilex× 'Nellie R. Stevens,' Nellie R. Stevens Holly
Ilex vomitoria, 'Pride of Houston,' 'Stokes Dwarf,' Yaupon Holly
Iris spp., Bearded Iris
Lagerstroemia indica, Crape Myrtle
Lantana spp., Lantana
Lantana montevidensis, Lavender Lantana
Lavandula spp., Lavender
Leucophyllum frutescens, Cenizo
Liatris spicata, Gayfeather
Miscanthus sinensis 'Variegatus,' Variegated Japanese Silver Grass
Monarda fistulosa, Wild Bergamont
Nandina domestica, Heavenly Bamboo
Nerium Oleander, Oleander
Oenothera Berlandieri, Mexican Evening Primrose
Oenothera missourensis, Ozark Sundrop
Pavonia spp., Rock Rose
Pennisetum setaceum, Fountain Grass
Plumbago spp., Plumbago
Portulaca oleracea, Purslane
Pyracantha spp., Firethorn
Rhaphiolepis indica, India Hawthorn
Rosa 'Don Juan'
Rosa banksia, Lady Banks' Rose
Rosa laevigata, Cherokee Rose
Rosa palustris, Swamp Rose

Rosmarinus officinalis, Rosemary
Rudbeckia spp., Black-Eyed Susan
Salvia spp., Sage
Santolina spp., Lavender Cotton
Schizachryrium scoparium, Little Bluestem
Sedum spp., Stonecrop
Verbena spp., Verbena
Yucca spp., Yucca

THE SOUTHEAST

TREES
Albizia julibrissin, Mimosa
Caesalpinia spp., Bird-of-Paradise
Catalpa speciosa, Catalpa
Cedrus Deodara, Deodar Cedar
Celtis laevigata, Mississippi Hackberry
Celtis occidentalis, Common Hackberry
Cercis canadensis, Redbud
Chilopsis linearis, Desert Willow
Cornus florida, Flowering Dogwood
Feijoa sellowiana, Pineapple Guava
Ficus carica, Edible Fig
Fraxinus pennsylvanica, Green Ash
Ginkgo biloba, Maidenhair Tree
Gymnocladus dioica, Coffee Tree
Ilex decidua, Possumhaw Holly
Ilex opaca, American Holly
Ilex vomitoria, Yaupon Holly
Juniperus silicicola, Southern Red Cedar
Lagerstroemia indica, Crape Myrtle
Liquidambar styraciflua, Sweet Gum
Magnolia grandiflora, Southern Magnolia
Myrica cerifera, Wax Myrtle
Pinus elliotti, Slash Pine
Pinus palustris, Longleaf Pine
Prunus caroliniana, Cherry Laurel

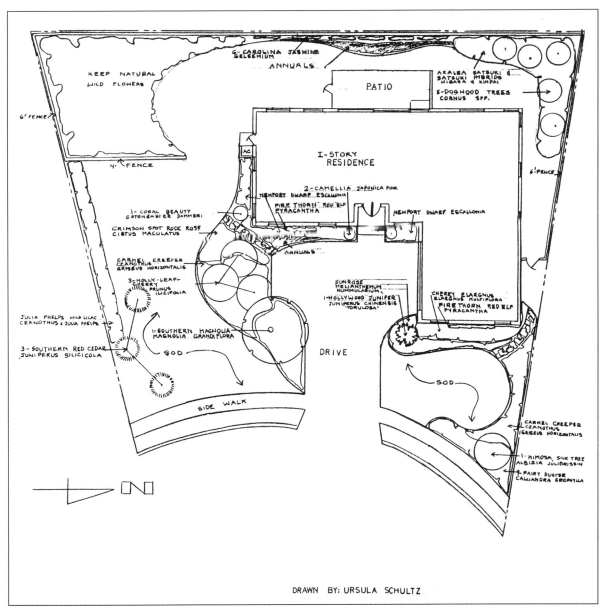

The labels in the plan:

6-CAROLINA JASMINE GELSEMIUM

ANNUALS

KEEP NATURAL WILD FLOWERS

PATIO

AZALEA SATSUKI & SATSUKI HIBRIDS HIGASA & KINPAI

6-DOGWOOD TREES CORNUS SPP.

6' FENCE

4' FENCE

AC

1-STORY RESIDENCE

6' FENCE

2-CAMELLIA JAPONICA PINK

NEWPORT DWARF ESCALLONIA

1- CORAL BEAUTY COTONEASTER DAMMERI

FIRE THORN RED ELF PYRACANTHA

NEWPORT DWARF ESCALLONIA

CRIMSON SPOT ROCK ROSE CISTUS MACULATUS

CARMEL CREEPER CEANOTHUS GRISEUS HORIZONTALIS

ANNUALS

3-HOLLY-LEAF-CHERRY PRUNUS ILICIFOLIA

SUN ROSE HELIANTHEMUM NUMMULARIUM

CHERRY ELAEGNUS ELAEGNUS MULTIFLORA

JULIA PHELPS WILD LILAC CEANOTHUS & JULIA PHELPS

1-HOLLYWOOD JUNIPER JUNIPERUS CHINENSIS 'TORULOSA'

FIRE THORN RED ELF PYRACANTHA

3 - SOUTHERN RED CEDAR JUNIPERUS SILICICOLA

1-SOUTHERN MAGNOLIA MAGNOLIA GRANDIFLORA

SOD

DRIVE

SOD

SIDE WALK

CARMEL CREEPER CEANOTHUS GRISEUS HORIZONTALIS

N

1 - MIMOSA, SILK TREE ALBIZIA JULIBRISSIN

FAIRY DUSTER CALLIANDRA ERIOPHYLLA

DRAWN BY: URSULA SCHULTZ

The Southeast.

	SHRUBS AND PERENNIALS
Quercus macrocarpa, Bur Oak	*Achillea millefolium,* Common Yarrow
Quercus palustris, Pin Oak	*Agapanthus africanus,* Lily of the Nile
Quercus Shumardii, Shumard Red Oak	*Agave americana,* Century Plant
Quercus stellata, Post Oak	*Antigonon leptopus,* Coral Vine
Quercus virginiana, Live Oak	*Aquilegia canadensis,* Wild Columbine
Robinia spp., Locust	*Artemisia ludoviciana,* Silver King Artemisia
Sambucus canadensis, American Elderberry	

Asclepias tuberosa, Butterfly Weed
Asparagus densiflorus
Aspidistra elatior, Cast-Iron Plant
Aster spp., Aster
Baptisia australis, False Indigo
Caesalpinia pulcherrima, Barbados Pride
Caladium spp., Caladium
Campsis radicans, Trumpet Creeper
Canna × *generalis,* Canna
Clematis paniculata, Sweet Autumn Clematis
Clytostoma callistegioides, Lavender Trumpet Vine
Convolvulus spp., Morning Glory
Coreopsis verticillata 'Moonbeam'
Cotoneaster spp., Cotoneaster
Distictis buccinatoria, Scarlet Trumpet Vine
Echinacea purpurea, Purple Coneflower
Gaillardia grandiflora, Blanketflower
Gelsimium sempervirens, Carolina Jasmine
Hamelia patens, Firebush
Helianthus Maximiliani, Maximilian Sunflower
Helleborus lividus corsicus, Corsican Hellebore
Hemerocallis spp., Day Lily
Hesperaloe parviflora, Red Yucca
Hibiscus rosa-sinensis, Chinese Hibiscus
Hippeastrum × *johnsonii,* Amaryllis
Ilex cornuta 'Burfordii,' Burford Holly
Ilex cornuta 'Rotunda,' Dwarf Chinese Holly
Ilex × 'Nellie R. Stevens,' Nellie R. Stevens Holly
Ilex vomitoria, 'Pride of Houston,' 'Stokes Dwarf,' Yaupon Holly
Iris spp., Bearded Iris
Lagerstroemia indica, Crape Myrtle
Lantana montividensis, Lavender Lantana
Lavandula spp., Lavender
Liatris spicata, Gayfeather

Miscanthus sinensis 'Variegatus,' Variegated Japanese Silver Grass
Monarda didyma, Bee Balm
Monarda fistulosa, Wild Bergamont
Nandina domestica, Heavenly Bamboo
Nerium Oleander, Oleander
Oenothera missourensis, Ozark Sundrop
Osmanthus fragrans, Sweet Olive
Pennisetum setaceum, Fountain Grass
Plumbago spp., Plumbago
Portulaca oleracea, Purslane
Pyracantha spp., Firethorn
Rhaphiolepis indica, India Hawthorn
Rosa 'Don Juan'
Rosa banksia, Lady Banks Rose
Rosa laevigata, Cherokee Rose
Rosa palustris, Swamp Rose
Rosmarinus officinalis, Rosemary
Rudbeckia spp., Black-Eyed Susan
Salvia spp., Sage
Santolina spp., Lavender Cotton
Schizachryium scoparium, Little Bluestem
Sedum spp., Stonecrop
Verbena spp., Verbena
Yucca spp., Yucca

THE EAST AND NORTHEAST

TREES

Acer palmatum, Japanese Maple
Acer rubrum, Red Maple
Catalpa speciosa, Catalpa
Cedrus atlantica, Atlas Cedar
Cedrus Deodara, Deodar Cedar
Cedrus libani, Cedar of Lebanon
Celtis occidentalis, Common Hackberry
Cercis canadensis, Redbud
Cornus florida, Flowering Dogwood

Fraxinus pennsylvanica, Green Ash
Gymnocladus dioica, Coffee Tree
Ilex opaca, American Holly
Liquidambar styraciflua, Sweet Gum
Prunus cistena, Dward Red Leaf Plum
Quercus macrocarpa, Bur Oak
Quercus palustris, Pin Oak
Quercus stellata, Post Oak
Sambucus canadensis, American Elderberry

SHRUBS AND PERENNIALS

Aquilegia canadensis, Wild Columbine
Asclepias tuberosa, Butterfly Weed
Aster spp., Aster
Baptisia australis, False Indigo
Bergenia cordifolia
Callicarpa japonica, Japanese Beautyberry
Campsis radicans, Trumpet Creeper
Cerastium tomentosum,
    Snow-in-the-Summer
Ceratostigma plumbaginoides, Dwarf
    Plumbago
Chrysanthemum morifolium,
    Chrysanthemum
Cotoneaster spp., Cotoneaster
Echinacea purpurea, Purple Coneflower
Echinops exaltatus, Globe Thistle
Hedera helix, English Ivy
Helianthus Maximiliani, Maximilian
    Sunflower
Hemerocallis spp., Day Lily
Ilex cornuta 'Burfordii,' Burford Holly
Ilex cornuta 'Rotunda,' Dwarf Chinese Holly
Ilex × 'Nellie R. Stevens,' Nellie R. Stevens
    Holly
Iris spp., Bearded Iris
Lavandula spp., Lavender
Liatris spicata, Gayfeather
Lonicera japonica, Japanese Honeysuckle

Monarda didyma, Bee Balm
Pyracantha spp., Firethorn
Taxus spp., Yew

FLORIDA

TREES

Albizia Lebbeck, Woman's Tongue Tree
Araucaria heterophylla, Norfolk Island Pine
Arecastrum Romanzoffianium, Queen Palm
Bauhinia spp., Orchid Tree
Bucida buceras, Black Olive
Bursera simaruba, Gumbo-Limbo Tree
Butia capitata, Pindo Palm
Caesalpinia spp., Bird-of-Paradise
Callistemon citrinus, Lemon Bottlebrush
Caryota mitis, Fishtail Palm
Chorisia speciosa, Floss Silk Tree
Dalbergia sissoo, Indian Rosewood
Eucalyptus spp., Eucalyptus
Feijoa sellowiana, Pineapple Guava
Grevillea robusta, Silk Oak Tree
Ilex decidua, Possumhaw Holly
Ilex vomitoria, Yaupon Holly
Jacaranda mimosifolia
Juniperus silicicola, Southern Red Cedar
Lagerstroemia indica, Crape Myrtle
Liquidambar styraciflua, Sweet Gum
Magnolia grandiflora, Southern Magnolia
Myrica cerifera, Wax Myrtle
Phoenix canariensis, Canary Island Date
    Palm
Phoenix reclinata, Senegal Date Palm
Pinus palustris, Longleaf Pine
Quercus virginiana, Live Oak
Sabal Palmetto, Cabbage Palm
Tabebuia spp., Trumpet Tree

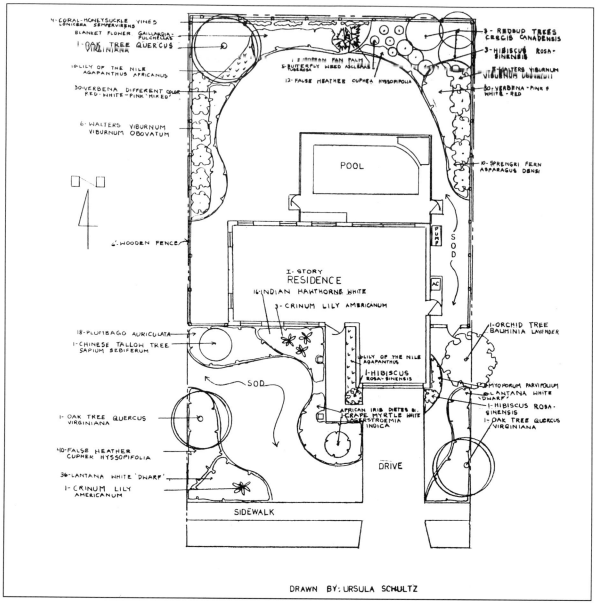

4-CORAL-HONEYSUCKLE VINES
LONICERA SEMPERVIRENS
BLANKET FLOWER GAILLARDIA-
PULCHELLAS
1-OAK TREE QUERCUS
VIRGINIANA

10-LILY OF THE NILE
AGAPANTHUS AFRICANUS

30-VERBENA DIFFERENT COLOR
RED-WHITE-PINK 'MIXED'

6-WALTERS VIBURNUM
VIBURNUM OBOVATUM

6'-WOODEN FENCE

18-PLUMBAGO AURICULATA

1-CHINESE TALLOW TREE
SAPIUM SEBIFERUM

1-OAK TREE QUERCUS
VIRGINIANA

40-FALSE HEATHER
CUPHER HYSSOPIFOLIA

36-LANTANA WHITE 'DWARF'

1-CRINUM LILY
AMERICANUM

1-EUROPEAN FAN PALM
5-BUTTERFLY WEED ASCLEAS
TUBEROSA
12-FALSE HEATHER CUPHEA HYSSOPIFOLIA

3-REDBUD TREES
CRECIS CANADENSIS
3-HIBISCUS ROSA-
SINENSIS
6-WALTERS VIBURNUM
VIBURNUM OBOVATUM
30-VERBENA-PINK &
WHITE-RED

10-SPRENGRI FERN
ASPARAGUS DENSI

POOL

SOD

PUMP
AC

1-STORY
RESIDENCE
16-INDIAN HAWTHORNE WHITE
3-CRINUM LILY AMERICANUM

1-ORCHID TREE
BAUHINIA LAVENDER

1-LILY OF THE NILE
AGAPANTHUS
1-HIBISCUS
ROSA-SINENSIS

5-MYOPORUM PARVIFOLIUM
6-LANTANA WHITE
'DWARF'
1-HIBISCUS ROSA-
SINENSIS
1-OAK TREE QUERCUS
VIRGINIANA

SOD

AFRICAN IRIS DIETES B.
1-CRAPE MYRTLE WHITE
LAGERSTROEMIA
INDICA

DRIVE

SIDEWALK

DRAWN BY: URSULA SCHULTZ

Florida.

Washingtonia robusta, Washington Palm	*Asparagus densiflorus*
Zamia floridana, Coontie	*Aspidistra elatior,* Cast-Iron Plant
	Beaucarnea recurvata, Ponytail Palm
SHRUBS AND PERENNIALS	*Bougainvillea* spp., Bougainvillea
Agapanthus africanus, Lily of the Nile	*Caesalpinia pulcherrima,* Barbados Pride
Agave americana, Century Plant	*Caladium* spp., Caladium
Antigonon leptopus, Coral Vine	*Campsis radicans,* Trumpet Creeper

Canna × *generalis*, Canna
Cistus spp., Rock Rose
Clematis paniculata, Sweet Autumn Clematis
Clytostoma callistegioides, Lavender Trumpet Vine
Convolvulus spp., Morning Glory
Cotoneaster spp., Cotoneaster
Cytisus spp., Broom Shrub
Distictis buccinatoria, Scarlet Trumpet Vine
Dizgotheca kerchoveana, False Aralia
Euphorbia pulcherrima, Poinsettia
Gelsimium sempervirens, Carolina Jasmine
Hamelia patens, Firebush
Hardenbergia violacea, Vine Lilac
Hibiscus rosa-sinensis, Chinese Hibiscus
Lagerstroemia indica, Crape Myrtle
Lantana spp., Lantana
Nandina domestica, Heavenly Bamboo
Nerium Oleander, Oleander
Rhaphiolepis indica, India Hawthorn
Rosa 'Don Juan'
Rosa laevigata, Cherokee Rose
Rosa palustris, Swamp Rose
Rosmarinus officinalis, Rosemary
Solandra maxima, Cup of Gold Vine
Yucca spp., Yucca

PLANTS FOR THE SEASIDE
(PLANTS WITH SALT TOLERANCE)

Arecastrum Romanzoffianum, Queen Palm
Atriplex spp., Saltbush
Baccharis pilularis, Coyote Bush
Bursera simaruba, Gumbo-Limbo Tree
Butia capitata, Pindo Palm
Carissa grandiflora 'Fancy'
Caryota mitis, Fishtail Palm
Casuarina spp., Australian Pine

Cistus spp., Rock Rose
Coprosma Kirkii
Cordyline indivisa, Blue Dracaena
Cytisus, Broom Shrub
Escallonia
Juniperus conferta 'Blue Pacific'
Nerium Oleander, Oleander
Phoenix canariensis, Canary Island Date Palm
Pinus eldarica, Eldarica Pine
Pinus halepensis, Aleppo Pine
Pinus radiata, Monterey Pine
Pinus roxburghii, Chir Pine
Parkinsonia aculeata, Jerusalem Thorn
Quercus virginiana, Live Oak
Sabal Palmetto, Cabbage Palm
Solandra maxima, Cup of Gold Vine

PLANTS FOR PARTIAL SHADE AND/OR SHADE

Abelia × *grandiflora*, Glossy Abelia
Acanthus mollis
Acer palmatum, Japanese Maple
Antigonon leptopus, Coral Vine
Aquilegia spp., Columbine
Asparagus densiflorus
Aspidistra elatior, Aspidistra
Aucuba japonica, Japanese Aucuba
Beaucarnea recurvata, Ponytail Palm
Bergenia cordifolia
Buxus microphylla japonica, Japanese Boxwood
Caladium spp.
Callicarpa japonica, Japanese Beautyberry
Campsis radicans, Trumpet Creeper
Carissa grandiflora, Natal Plum

Ceratostigma plumbaginoides, Dwarf
   Plumbago
Cestrum nocturnum, Night-Blooming
   Jasmine
Clematis paniculata, Sweet Autumn Clematis
Clytostoma callistegioides, Lavender Trumpet
   Vine
Codiaeum variegatum, Croton
Coleonema album, White Breath-of-Heaven
Convolvulus Cneorum, Bush Morning Glory
Coprosma Kirkii
Crinum bulbispermum, Crinum Lily
Elaeagnus pungens, Silverberry
Genista spp., Broom
Hedera helix, English Ivy
Helleborus foetidus
Helleborus lividus corsicus, Corsican
   Hellebore
Heteromeles arbutifolia
Ilex spp., Holly
Juniperus spp., Juniper
Lavandula spp., Lavender
Liriope muscari
Lonicera japonica, Japanese Honeysuckle
Mahonia spp.
Monarda didyma
Nandina domestica, Heavenly Bamboo
Pavonia spp., Rock Rose
Pennisetum setaceum, Fountain Grass
Plumbago spp.
Pittosporum tobira
Saxifraga × arendsii, Rockfolis
Taxus spp., Yew

NATIVE PLANT AND WILDFLOWER SOCIETIES OF THE UNITED STATES

National Council of State
Garden Clubs, Inc.
Operation Wildflower
P.O. Box 860
Pocasset, MA 02559-0860

National Wildflower Research Center
2600 F.M. 973 N
Austin, TX 78725-4201
512-929-3600

The National Wildflower Research Center publishes the *Wildflower Handbook,* an exhaustive reference to native plant societies, conservation agencies, nurseries and other sources for wildflower seed and plants, and landscape designers who work with wildflowers and/or native plants. It's about $12.95 at press time.

American Wildflower Society
Bluet Meadow
17 Le Clair Terrace
Chicopee, MA 01013

Alabama
The Alabama Wildflower Society
c/o George Wood
11120 Ben Clements Road
Northport, AL 35476

Alaska
Alaska Native Plant Society
P.O. Box 141613
Anchorage, AK 99514

Arizona
Arizona Native Plant Society
P.O. Box 41206
Tucson, AZ 85717

Arkansas
Arkansas Native Plant Society
Route 2 Box 256BB
Mena, AR 71953

California
California Native Plant Society
909 12th Street
Suite 116
Sacramento, CA 95814

Colorado
Colorado Native Plant Society
P.O. Box 200
Fort Collins, CO 80522

Florida
Florida Native Plant Society
P.O. Box 680008
Orlando, FL 32868

Idaho
Idaho Native Plant Society
P.O. Box 9451
Boise, ID 83707

Illinois
Illinois Native Plant Society
Forest Glen Preserve
Route 1 Box 495A
Westville, IL 61883

Kansas
Kansas Wildflower Society
Mulvane Art Center
Washburn University
Topeka, KS 66621

Kentucky
Kentucky Native Plant Society
Department of Biological Sciences
Eastern Kentucky University
Richmond, KY 40475

Louisiana
Acadiana Native Plant Society
637 Girard Park Drive
Lafayette, LA 70503

Louisiana Project Wildflower
c/o Lafayette Natural History Museum
637 Girard Park Drive
Lafayette, LA 70503

Massachusetts
New England Wild Flower Society
Garden in the Woods
Hemenway Road
Framingham, MA 01701

Michigan
Michigan Botanical Club
Matthaei Botanic Gardens
1800 North Dixboro Road
Ann Arbor, MI 48105

The Wildflower Association of Michigan
P.O. Box 80527
Lansing, MI 48908-0527

Minnesota
Minnesota Native Plant Society
220 Biological Science Center
1445 Gortner Avenue
St. Paul, MN 55108

Mississippi
Mississippi Native Plant Society
P.O. Box 2151
Starkville, MS 39759

Missouri
Missouri Native Plant Society
P.O. Box 6612
Jefferson City, MO 65102

Montana
Montana Native Plant Society
P.O. Box 992
Bozeman, MT 59771

Nevada
Northern Nevada Native Plant Society
P.O. Box 8965
Reno, NV 89507

New Jersey
New Jersey Native Plant Society
P.O. Box 1295
Morristown, NJ 07962-1295

New Mexico
Native Plant Society of New Mexico
P.O. Box 5917
Santa Fe, NM 87502

North Carolina
North Carolina Wild Flower
Preservation Society
c/o North Carolina Botanical Garden
CB#3375, UNC-CH
Chapel Hill, NC 27599-3375

Ohio
Ohio Native Plant Society
5 Louise Drive
Chagrin Falls, OH 44022

Oklahoma
Oklahoma Native Plant Society
2435 South Peoria Avenue
Tulsa, OK 74114

Oregon
Native Plant Society of Oregon
652 West 10th, #1
Eugene, OR 97402

Rhode Island
Rhode Island Wild Plant Society
12 Sanderson Road
Smithfield, RI 02917

South Carolina
Wildflower Alliance of South Carolina
P.O. Box 12181
Columbia, SC 29211

Tennessee
Tennessee Native Plant Society
P.O. Box 856
Sewanee, TN 37375-0856

Texas
El Paso Native Plant Society
c/o James F. George
7137 Gran Vida
El Paso, TX 79912

Native Plant Society of Texas
P.O. Box 891
210 West 8th Street
Suite A
Georgetown, TX 78627

Utah
Utah Native Plant Society
P.O. Box 520041
Salt Lake City, UT 84152-0041

Virginia
Virginia Native Plant Society
P.O. Box 844
Annandale, VA 22003

Washington
Washington Native Plant Society
Department of Botany, KB-15
University of Washington
Seattle, WA 98195

Wyoming
Wyoming Native Plant Society
P.O. Box 1471
Cheyenne, WY 82003-1471

XERISCAPE™ GARDENING/WATER CONSERVATION RESOURCES

There are a lot of resources available to the home gardener both on a community and national level. For example, water utility companies/authorities have programs, pamphlets, contests, and more to encourage water conservation in the home or business landscape. Write or call your local water agency and see what materials they have. I have listed a few here, but there are many more. Beyond that, there are national groups, botanical gardens, local clubs, state extension programs, etc. to offer help and guidance.

National Xeriscape Council, Inc.
P.O. Box 767936
Roswell, GA 30076-7936

Seeks to educate about Xeriscape™-type gardening throughout the country—and worldwide. Helps sponsor and encourage many community Xeriscape™ landscaping programs, as well as putting out an informa-tional quarterly newsletter. Individual memberships are available, as are municipal and professional affiliations. A good source of up-to-date information on water-wise landscaping. Send $3.00 to the above address for an information packet.

National Council of
State Garden Clubs, Inc.
4401 Magnolia Avenue
St. Louis, MO 63110

Many garden clubs are taking water conservation as their theme, and they are sometimes a good place to start for information and help. Most cities have garden clubs, and the National Council can give additional information.

Arizona Municipal Water Users
Association
4041 North Central Avenue
Suite 900
Phoenix, AZ 85012

Has several handy and informative pamphlets free to the public on water-use and landscaping for Arizona. Titles available include: "Water Wise Guidebook for Desert Lawns," "Xeriscape—A New Look for Arizona Gardens," "Plants for the Desert Southwest," and "A Summer Lawn Watering Guide." Write to the above address for further information.

City of Atlanta
Department of Water
68 Mitchell Street SW
Atlanta, GA 30335

Has water-conservation booklets available.

City of Austin Environmental and
Conservation Service Department
Water Conservation Program
206 East Ninth Street
Austin, TX 78701
512-499-3500

A source of water-conservation information
for Austin residents.

Randolph G. Harmon
c/o Birmingham Water Works
3600 First Avenue North
Birmingham, AL 35222

Has put together a home-use water-
conservation kit and provides water-
conservation tips for the home garden.

Denver Water
Office of Conservation
1600 West 12th Avenue
Denver, CO 80254
Conservation Hotline: 303-628-6343

Has a Xeriscape™ packet available that includes several information pamphlets. New
pamphlets of note are "Great Systems," on
automatic watering systems, and "Great
Grasses," on water-conserving alternatives
to Kentucky bluegrass for Colorado
gardeners.

El Paso Water Utilities
Water Conservation Department
P.O. Box 511
El Paso, TX 79961
915-594-5508

Besides information on Xeriscape™-
type design, this department sponsors

a Xeriscape™-style garden contest, the
Accent-Sun Country Contest, for great
gardens with low-water-use plants and/or
natives.

Water Conservation
El Paso County
Texas Agricultural Extension Service
1030 North Zaragosa Road, Suite A
El Paso, TX 79907

Excellent source of information for El Paso
residents, given El Paso's challenging climate, so different from the rest of the state.

Charles F. Lummis Home and Garden
Historical Society of Southern California
200 East Avenue 43
Los Angeles, CA 90031
213-222-0546

The two-acre garden and grounds of the his-
toric Lummis house is a drought-tolerant
garden featuring the plants that work in
Southern California. Many of the plants
used are colorful California natives. Of interest is the yarrow (*Achillea millefolium*)
meadow that offers an alternative to the
traditional turfgrass yard—and needs little
mowing.

Pinellas County Cooperative
Extension Service
12175 125th Street North
Largo, FL 34644
813-588-8110

Has an established (six years old)
Xeriscape™ garden on display with three
zones. Plantings are constantly being added

and tested, so it's a good source of drought-tolerant plant information for Floridians.
San Antonio Botanical Center
555 Funston Place
San Antonio, TX 78209
512-821-5115

Has an established Xeriscape™-design garden as part of the botanical garden.

San Diego County Water Authority
3211 Fifth Avenue
San Diego, CA 92103
619-297-3399

Will send water conservation information to interested gardeners, including a pamphlet on drought-tolerant plants for San Diego water-thrifty gardens.

Ursula E. Schultz
Landscape Design Consultant
P.O. Box 7634
St. Petersburg, FL 33734-7634

Specializes in Xeriscape™-type, drought-tolerant garden designs with detailed yet simple-to-follow landscape plans. Familiar with many regions' plant needs.

Seattle Water Department
Conservation Information Line:
206-233-7915

South Florida Management District
P.O. Box 24680
West Palm Beach, FL 33416-24680
407-686-8800

Besides a community Xeriscape program, has copies of the "Florida Xeriscape Law" (the first statewide Xeriscape ordinance) available upon written request.
Tucson Botanical Gardens
2150 North Alvernon Way
Tucson, AZ 85712

Includes the Xeriscape and Solar Demonstration Garden.

Water Smart
Texas Agricultural Extension Service
Texas A&M University
College Station, TX 77843

An educational program sponsored by the Texas Agricultural Extension Service that encourages efficient water use both in the garden and in the home. They put out a "Water Smart Distribution Kit" that includes tips on how to conserve water, a rain gauge, lawn grass information, and a handy log. The kit is available in hardware and garden supply stores. Texas residents can call their local Extension Service for more information.

Zilker Botanical Gardens
Xeriscape Garden
2220 Barton Springs Road
Zilker Park
Austin, TX 78746
512-477-8672

A demonstration garden more than five years old with recent new plantings. The gardens are managed by the Austin Area Garden Council.

WATER SYSTEMS INFORMATION

Most water systems companies and hardware stores have guides on how to install and operate the systems. Ask at your local hardware or garden supply store if they have any information, so that you can plan before you install. Here are a few of the companies and/or guides that are available.

Irrigation Catalog
Gardener's Supply Company
128 Intervale Road
Burlington, VT 05401
1-802-863-1700

Gardener's Supply Company puts out an irrigation catalog featuring up-to-date listings of their water-efficient irrigation systems, from soaker hoses and drip systems to rain barrels—so that you can collect your own water and store it.

Moisture Master
610 South 80th Avenue
Phoenix, AZ 85043
602-936-0401

Makers of the soaker hose system discussed in Chapter 7.

Rain Bird Sprinkler Mfg. Corp.
145 North Grand Avenue
Glendora, CA 91740
1-800-247-3782

Write or ask at a local retailer for Rain Bird's "3-Step Drip Planning Guide," a pamphlet on their drip watering system. Raindrip, Inc.

"Drip Watering Made Easy"
21305 Itasca Street
Chatsworth, CA 91311
1-800-225-3747 (CA only)
1-800-544-3747 (outside CA)

Raindrip puts out a detailed and handy guide to their low-volume drip watering systems: how it works, planning, parts, accessories, converting an existing system, etc. It's available at hardware and garden supply stores for around $1.98 (at press time).

Index